TRANSFORMING EMOTIONS:

Using your emotions to transform others and remain safe

An Ericksonian Approach

Dr. John D. Lentz

ISBN: 1983971170
ISBN 13: 9781983971174

ACKNOWLEDGEMENTS

Jennifer B. Chrisman M.Div. LMFT-A edited this volume and gave helpful comments as well as invaluable encouragement.

There are many others who deserve recognition who have contributed in all sorts of ways, including folks who have given their encouragement for this volume.

My wife Debra deserves a lot of acknowledgement because of how she helps me by being so steadfast, dependable, and kind. She often overlooks my mistakes and continues to help.

TABLE OF CONTENTS

Acknowledgements iii
Introduction ix

Chapter 1 An Emotional Alchemy of Sorts 1
Chapter 2 A Useful Way of Thinking about Emotions 7
Chapter 3 The Problem Points to Strengths and Abilities
You May Not Have Realized You Have 11
Chapter 4 The Problem of Toxic Emotions 20
Chapter 5 We Learn the Most Profound Lessons
through Experiences 26
Chapter 6 How this System Works 33
Chapter 7 Overt and Covert Emotions 45
Chapter 8 Trade in Your Codependency for a Strength 50
Chapter 9 Sexual Feelings Are Not Always About Sex,
Even if They Feel that Way 56
Chapter 10 Protecting Yourself from Other People's
Sexual Feelings 63
Chapter 11 Alchemy for Other People's Guilt 71
Chapter 12 Your Feelings Can Be a Window Into
Another Person's Soul 77
Chapter 13 Changing How You Feel 82

"At the center of every fairy tale lay a truth that gave the story it's power."
Susan Wiggs, <u>The You I Never Knew</u>

"Fairy tales since the beginning; of reported time, and perhaps earlier, have been a means to conquer the terrors of mankind through metaphor."
Jack Zipes

"I don't know these stories as well as they know me, I've discovered."
Joan Gould

"To win one hundred victories in one hundred battles is not the highest skill. To subdue the enemy without fighting is the highest skill."
Sun Tzu

"A dog at play has the mind of a wise martial arts master, a mind capable of perfect focus."
Anonymous

INTRODUCTION

Once upon a time there was a man who was going about his usual business when he discovered a goose that laid golden eggs. He was very excited and thought about all the things he should do with this wonderful discovery. Until he began to have doubts. The doubts he had were serious doubts...you know, the type that keep you up at night. He began to fight with himself. The trouble began because part of him didn't believe the eggs were really golden, and another part didn't believe that the goose actually laid the eggs. But a still other part wanted to believe in this goose and even the golden eggs. He wanted something magical in his life, but he reasoned this couldn't happen as it went against everything that he believed and could see and touch.

The fight inside of himself wanted proof. He reasoned that he could tell if the eggs were golden by taking a scraping to a Jeweler, so he did, hoping to calm the internal debate. He was disappointed. It didn't fix anything because once he knew the eggs were golden he still doubted. Now that he knew that they were not just painted, the doubt had only moved to wondering where they came from. Since his logic told him that the goose couldn't have laid them, he then wondered how the eggs got into the nest. He reasoned that everyone knows that geese don't lay golden eggs, except in fairy the tales. Now where was it that he had studied about fairy tales and their multilevel communication? He remembered that fairy tales communicate messages in a symbolic way that are difficult to communicate any other way. Then he came back to reality and reasoned that the eggs couldn't have been from the goose, so he began to wonder if someone was trying to trick him in some elaborate scheme. So he became suspicious of everyone trying to trick him. However, since he remembered in the fairy tale that the person who found the goose lost everything because of greed, he decided to avoid spending any of the golden eggs. In fact, he simply melted them down and gave the gold to charities. That way he wasn't dependent upon the money and he was able to do lots of good no matter what else happened. If someone was tricking him, he would have the last laugh.

At first he was convinced that others knew something that he didn't know and they were keeping the truth from him. It didn't take too long to discover that this line of thinking wasn't helping a lot because he started to become more and more suspicious. Actually he started becoming suspicious of everyone. In fact, as he became more and more suspicious people began to avoid him. They could feel his suspiciousness and they didn't like it. Their pulling back made him even more convinced he was right. He just knew that someone was tricking him. His wife began to complain that he was becoming difficult to even talk with. While his logic hadn't helped him much with this whole business, he still kept at it with his usual logical style. In fact, this time he realized that his suspiciousness wasn't going to help him unravel the mystery. So he reasoned with himself and eventually stopped being suspicious and simply sat with the ambiguity of not knowing where the eggs came from. Now, if you have ever tried to stop being suspicious, you know how amazing this man was. He had simply decided to stop giving in to his fears and made peace with them.

Later he decided that since he didn't know how they eggs got there and wasn't likely to be able to find out, he would appreciate them whether they kept coming or stopped. Finally, he began to count on the eggs even if he didn't know how they got into the nest and even if he didn't really believe that the goose laid the eggs. He remembered in the fairy tale that the person who found the goose lost everything because of greed.   He didn't want to be made fun of or become dependent upon the eggs, so he decided to avoid spending any of the golden eggs. In fact, he simply kept melting them down and gave the gold to charities. That way he wasn't dependent upon the money and he was able to do lots of good no matter what else happened. He was quite proud of the fact that he had done better than the original golden goose handler. He was managing the gold quite well. After a short while he realized that if people knew that he was the one giving or having that much gold he was going to be overrun with people wanting things and he wouldn't want to have to say no to his wife or any family member who would ask him for money so he simply gave the gold anonymously. He was glad that he hadn't told anyone and so it was easy to keep his own secret.

During this entire time the man treated the goose as if it was laying the golden eggs. No matter how suspicious, or doubtful he was he always treated the goose as if all the eggs came from her. It was a way he was able to be respectful to the goose. He had become quite fond of the goose. The Goose seemed almost magical, whether it was really laying golden eggs or not. Much later in life, he realized that the real magic was how he treated the goose. His treatment of the goose is what had made so much of a difference, but that is getting ahead of ourselves. He still didn't know how the eggs got into the nest but he knew that the goose appreciated that he treated her well. They grew close and became quite fond of each other. At least that was what happened after the man decided to stop being so suspicious and just appreciate what he was receiving no matter what, and to appreciate the goose just because she was so important to him as an individual whether she had anything to do with the eggs or not. He became fond of her and loved her. His loving the goose changed his life. He began to relate more effectively toward everyone he had contact with and even became more self-affirming. He and the goose loved each other and lived happily ever after, even though there were lots of other people in their lives, they continued to love and respect each other. It was really uncanny because as he loved the goose and gave the golden eggs away in his stealthy way, he felt better about himself and it started effecting his relationships. He got a raise at work, and people began to like him more and more. He seemed to have an air of confidence that was always there. As for his wife, she started loving him even more and their marriage became a standard for people everywhere that knew them. The depth of their relationship was clear and you could almost feel the closeness they had. Everywhere the couple went, people commented on how loving they seemed to be toward each other. People began to simply think that the man's ability to be so confident was because of his good relationship. He never told anyone any differently, and he simply lived happily ever after.

This book is written in an unusual way. It is written to give you back options, strengths, and abilities that you may not even know that you had; in fact, you may not even realize you want or need them yet. You have lived with feelings your whole life and you may not have even considered that you have more options than you think, because you may have assumed that everyone has the same struggles and that everyone has the same emotions. Whether you recognized that there may be things about feelings that you didn't yet know or not, you are about to discover some options you have that you may not have known or didn't know how to use so easily. As you read the book you may notice odd ways of using tense or voicing. It is written primarily so that it makes sense to the part of your brain that focuses upon experiences, rather than logic. It was written intentionally to offer you experiences that can alter your options so that you will simply have and feel more powerful, capable, and knowledgeable even if you don't understand all that has been said from the double and perhaps triple meanings.

It has been written to be helpful emotionally to you as much as possible first, and second to give you cognitive options. As such, it may not always read in usual ways. The written word is limited in its scope and cannot convey all the meanings and nuances that personal interactions convey. So in order to provide resources that are not primarily logical, some other means need to be employed. What follows are my attempts to do that in various ways while also conveying messages that are addressed to the logical part of your brain.

If you don't at first understand the fairy tale about the goose and the golden eggs, then just let the ideas and the fairy tale continue to be with you. When you make a connection and can appreciate it even more, you can feel even more respect for yourself because you will have also achieved a milestone.

CHAPTER 1

AN EMOTIONAL ALCHEMY OF SORTS

*"All magic is a science of sorts. It employs
knowledge and principles in ways to alter
perception for a particular purpose."*

Anonymous

*"Alchemy is still practiced but we call it other things.
The folks who understand alchemy know it never really
needed to make gold out of lead except as a metaphor."*

Anonymous

Wouldn't it be nice to have a way to keep yourself safe from having very unpleasant emotions? Wouldn't it be useful if you could change how you feel and invite the feelings that you want? While of course that is possible you may not have realized how easy it actually is. Did you ever dream as a child that you could change your feelings and change the feelings of others around you? Even if you didn't it is more possible in an indirect way than you may have ever thought possible. If you were ever bullied by others or picked on by someone, knowing how to protect yourself from emotions that are communicated in words would also be useful. It is more possible than you may have ever dreamed.

You probably didn't even know that you needed or wanted to know how to deal with emotions that have bothered you. Usually when something isn't bothering us we don't really think about it, until it bothers us again. You may not even have known that there were easier ways of coping with emotions that have bothered you in the past or ways to keep them from bothering you in the future. Since we all live with our emotions and have our whole lives, most all of us figure that we know as well as anyone else how to deal with them. It would seem like someone offering to teach you how to use your right hand. This book is written because the short cuts that I have learned over the years have proved very helpful to people and they wanted these techniques shared with you. I am not just talking about the feelings that have bothered you because you didn't know what to do with them, but also the feelings of others that you may not have known what to do with either. Who hasn't wondered how to cope with the intense emotions of friends, family or even strangers? Who hasn't wanted to know better ways of coping with ourselves emotionally?

One definition I found on the internet of alchemy is "a seemingly magical process of transformation, creation, or combination." This book is about teaching what amounts to an alchemy of emotions. As such, you will learn to utilize your emotions and the emotions of others in a strategic way to impact and influence others and to keep yourself safe. You will also begin to recognize new ways of influencing people. This book is designed to give you options and point out strengths that you didn't know you had as well as transform problems into opportunities. It may feel as if they are new options but you had them all along, you just didn't know it. Any similarities to other styles of emotional self- help or psychology is accidental. These concepts can, of course, be used with any or all other forms of therapy, and would add to any of them.

Not only do most of us have difficulty from time to time with our own emotions we also have to cope with the emotions of others. Most of us recognize that strong emotions such as fear in a crowed place can impact everyone. That is one of the reasons it isn't legal to shout fire in a theater or crowed place, or talk about bombs in airports. Strong emotions can be passed and they can cause a general panic. It is what happens to the economy when there is a down turn. It is also what happens when a team loses and everyone in the community had been rooting for the team. These sad feelings are not just because of identifying with the team, but from being in the community as well.

We also benefit from positive emotions. When you fell in love, your partner's love impacted you and your love impacted them. When the economy was strong you probably benefited. When you went to a ball game and were immersed in the emotions of excitement, you probably enjoyed yourself. When you were in a worshiping community you benefited from the emotions of the other worshipers. Emotions enrich our lives. It is, perhaps, because they are so important to us that when things are not going well they can cause us so much grief.

Our culture doesn't universally recognize that emotions can be passed between people, let alone that they often are more easily passed than passing germs. The toxic emotions of others have impacted you in lots of ways and in numerous places. They have given you trouble that you may not have recognized wasn't from you or how to deal with it once it became yours. You may not have recognized that it isn't just folks who are described as codependent or emotionally sensitive that get stuck with emotions that they didn't ask for and didn't have anything to do with generating.

There have been times that you picked up someone else's bad mood and then took it out on someone you love. Then when they retaliated against you, you may not have even know what happened. You have also been infected with toxic emotions that had lingering effects, disrupting your feelings of safety, calm, happiness, or wellbeing.

You probably have had occasions when you were having a good day, when all of a sudden you didn't even know how come you were not feeling so good. You may have begun to feel irritated, hurt, angry, or jealous. You may have been suddenly more impatient, anxious, or fearful. You could even have discovered that you were feeling fine, then seemingly out of the blue you began feeling blue, anxious, or inadequate.

Most of us have enough difficulty dealing with our own feelings. We struggle with stress, we fear that we aren't enough and never will be, or we notice our feelings of anger, sadness, shame, or loneliness that we don't really know how to cope with.

What if you were to begin to recognize when you have been infected with others emotions that caused you to have to deal with things that you didn't want to or that made your life more difficult? Have you ever wondered how come some people cheat on their spouses when they seemed to be in love? Have you struggled with anxiety in crowds and not known what to do with the emotions? Have you felt inspired by the faith, confidence, or integrity of another person? Have you wondered how some folks can be ok, even though they cope with a whirlwind of emotions? What about wanting to gently help others who you knew were struggling and you didn't have the right words?

If the answer is yes to any of the above then you may want to know more about emotional martial arts so that you can not only stay safe, but even use emotions as a tool for helping others as well as helping yourself.

That is the point of this book. It is offering to you ways to be safe emotionally when you are around others as well as when you are by yourself. There are lots of times that we encounter feelings of others that cause us no problems, and then other times they do.

As a therapist and chaplain I saw people all the time who were blindsided by emotions that caught them off guard. I saw folks get hurt and then hurt others because they didn't know how to cope with the strong emotions they were feeling. I have seen people make major mistakes that cost them their careers, homes, friends, and even the loyalty of their families because of not knowing how to deal with emotions. I have seen others change their lives in powerful and positive ways that were and remain inspiring because of emotions.

I would love to say that all of my struggles about emotions and how to cope with them was for others. It hasn't been. I have struggled in major ways that I didn't know what to do with: experiencing the shame and loneliness of being an only child whose mother became sick and then died, having no one to talk to about what happened to my mother, and coping with the multitude of emotions that seemed to flood the very campus at the women's prison where I worked for over 23 years. During these struggles when I didn't know what to do, I sought out answers. I was always learning. In many ways this book represents the struggle to find many of the answers to the questions that plagued me for so long, answers that would have been so helpful had I known them long ago.

While there are religious books of both the west and east that will tell us how to cope with emotions, often the path is long and difficult. It takes time to learn the rituals, and personal ability to control emotions from those religious practices. Modern life is difficult and moves at a fast pace. Having quick ways of keeping us safe as well as coping with emotions seems like a utopia. It isn't. It isn't even that difficult if you know how to do it. However, we are going to be dealing with emotions without addressing a religion or other practices, so it isn't going to take that much effort.

For a very long time I have been discovering answers that made my life and the lives of others much easier because I have looked at options that we normally don't explore. Growing up as an only child who was mostly on his own by the age of 9 made me look for answers in some unconventional ways. While I looked for answers I was also learning to look outside of the normal ways of searching and asking questions. I knew that the people around me didn't have the answers I sought, so I went to important writers from the past in a variety of fields. Lots of people have done that out of desperation, and most of us have discovered things that have been useful. I learned to look at problems from as many different perspectives as I could. When I did that with emotions, I discovered things that revolutionized people's lives. As I started on this book, I realized that I have been on this journey for a very long time. Some of the learnings that I gathered came from events from long ago that I hadn't yet realized how to understand.

Reading neuroscience today and beginning to understand options that we have but which no one realized years ago has answered many questions for me. I hope that you too will appreciate these as much as others have. The intention is for this book to be short so that you can read all of it and then become more creative in your own capacity to utilize these paths. My intention is to invite you to recognize your strengths and abilities that you may not have noticed in dealing with emotions that have been a problem for you in the past.

CHAPTER 2

A USEFUL WAY OF THINKING ABOUT EMOTIONS

"What logic didn't get us into, logic won't get us out of."

Shaker Proverb

When I was almost finished with the book, I told Jeff Zeig, PhD about it. He asked me what my definition of emotion was. I was dumbstruck. I thought everybody knows what emotions are, right? We all have them, and as humans we all have the same feelings, don't we? I was wrong. We do have the same visceral experiences; however, we don't all interpret them the same. While we all live with them so much that we don't really think about them, emotions have a powerful impact on our life. We mostly tend to treat emotions as if they are biological and universal. While the visceral experiences may be universal the interpretation of them is anything but universal, it isn't even close. Dr. Zeig's definition of emotion is a useful one that I think you will appreciate because it distinguishes them from moods and attitudes. His ability to use words precisely is extraordinary, and well deserved. I am indebted to him for his clarity. His ideas about emotions, moods, etc. are in his book "The Induction of Hypnosis: An Ericksonian Elicitation Approach".

Dr Zeig's definition is, "Emotions are fleeting visceral experiences that are directional." Fleeting visceral experiences implies that they are not here to stay. Some form of them may seem as if they can't be gotten rid of or changed but that is where the book comes in. Many times there are things a person does that perpetuate a feeling to re-occur. That is good news because it also means there are things we can do to stop them, change them and even to invite them. That the visceral experience is directional refers to the fact that emotions tend to invite us to move closer or to move away.

Emotions tend to cause us to leave places at times. A friend told a story about a camera man in a recent war zone who was known as being almost psychic. While practically no one believed he really was psychic, no one who was with him ever was hurt by an Improvised Explosive device. Yet, bombs like that had killed many people, and in fact were responsible for the majority of casualties. Everyone knew how dangerous the roadside bombs were. He somehow always knew where they were and avoided them. Most folks treated his idiosyncratic psychic ability as something like a rabbit's foot until one day when they were filming and he said, " Stop, it is time to leave here right now. " He was so serious that no one doubted him, and everyone threw themselves and their gear into a car, and began speeding away. Just as they were leaving and going as fast as they could possibly drive, they noticed trip wires attached to garbage on the side of the road and the bombs began exploding right where they had been. Had they stayed any later they would have been doomed. His emotions had literally saved them. Emotions are that important in giving us information and direction to go in order to be safe. Many of us have had a feeling that helped keep us ok. It may have been to jump, leave, move, or run, and it helped us.

On the other hand there are those times when we are the camera man helping others, and times when we are the people being helped. We are drawn to people at times so we can help them and others because they can help us. Usually, it is a two way street where both of us help the other, but it is fun to attempt to do more good than comes back to you. It is a fun way to live because it means that we are always looking for someone who we can be of assistance to. Once, I was able to help a woman I know only casually with two very important things in her life because I noticed that she was sitting by herself. I asked if I could sit with her and she began pouring out what was bothering her. Lots of other folks passed her up, but since I tend to notice things like someone's moods I chose to see if I could help. As we parted she hugged me and was genuinely appreciative.

However helpful emotions are in telling us to leave situations that are dangerous or drawing us to people and places that are good for us, emotions are fleeting.

Moods are not emotions. Moods are calcified states according to Dr. Zeig. As such, moods tend to be based upon the attitudes, beliefs, and visceral experiences that have been repeatedly defined in habitual ways. For example, the complex emotions that come from the moods and calcified beliefs of smokers perpetuate their smoking. When they realize that the feelings they have been interpreting as urges or cravings to smoke are actually their body healing from the damage they have been doing by smoking, they often begin to see the process of smoking differently. So how a person interprets their feelings and the beliefs surrounding those interpretations may make a huge difference in how and what they do based upon the feelings.

The more a person wants to avoid a certain emotion, get rid of it, or never have it again, the more the emotion seems to grow, becomes more of a problem, and almost never leaves.

On the other hand, an emotion that a person wants to experience may become very fleeting. We have all had emotions that we wish we could call up at will and they are more easily created than most people recognize. Wanting to stay in love can become like that. It can become so difficult to achieve because the emotion has left and doesn't seem to return. Some folks believe that means they should divorce. Sometimes the problem is that they were trying too hard to evoke a certain emotion rather than allowing it to come by evoking situations that are likely to create those feelings. This process is easier than most people think.

Emotions may be fleeting, and how we treat them may make getting away from them or altering our moods more difficult because of things that we have taken for granted.

CHAPTER 3

THE PROBLEM POINTS TO STRENGTHS AND ABILITIES YOU MAY NOT HAVE REALIZED YOU HAVE

"There is a saying in Tibetan, 'Tragedy should be utilized as a source of strength'."

Dalai Lama XIV

Jane: What do you mean that I have been feeling other's feelings? What are you saying about me?

Therapist: That you are really intelligent and that you are very aware.

Jane: That sounds like some science fiction or 'woo woo' beliefs.

Therapist: It is usually referred to as mirroring neurons and it has been researched a lot since it was first discovered.

Jane: You mean it really is possible to feel the feelings of others?

Therapist: Not only is it possible, but it is what has been a problem for you and lots of other folks.

Jane: How does it work? I mean how is it possible?

Therapist: Well that is speculative and debated. We don't really know, but we do know that it happens and you have been doing it.

Jane: So my feeling anxious isn't mine?

Therapist: Well it isn't all yours. I don't really know how much is yours and how much is theirs. My guess is about 10 to 15% is yours and 85% is theirs.

Jane: How do you know?

Therapist: In my presence you are calm and seemed to pick up my calm very easily. Your 10-15% has probably been in part because you didn't know this and you have believed it was all yours. If you can be calm with me it tells me you pick up feelings and that you aren't generating it yourself. Some of your anxiety comes the old fashioned way by paying attention to finding fault inside of yourself instead of noticing what is going on in the environment.

Jane: So how do I stop?

Therapist: Before we get to that, let's have you notice your feelings and monitor them over this next week. That way you will be able to recognize what I have told you is true. It will be better for your success to stop feeling what others are feeling if you realize it and have personal experience that it is true. Just believing me isn't really helpful until you see it and sense it yourself. Notice how you are feeling before someone comes into the room, and then notice how you feel after they leave, factoring in what they may have said while they were with you. If they haven't talked about anything that is overly scary or bothersome but you still notice feeling differently after they have left than before they came in, then you know you were probably picking up their feelings.

Jane: You aren't going to tell me today are you?

Therapist: No.

Jane: It is a lot to grasp at once.

Therapist: That is right and I know you will understand it best when you can have personal experiences that you know happened.

That is how we change. Our understanding of things changes and then we experience things differently.

I don't really want to go any further on this day because I know that sometimes too much change in one day can be overwhelming, especially regarding how we have been seeing the world. Such overloading can cause a person to reject the whole idea. It is a radical thing to realize that you have been feeling what others feel, and yet that is exactly what happens a lot of the time in a lot of situations. Sometimes these felt feelings are good, like when we go to ball games, festivals, and religious gatherings. We like those things in part because we can feel the feelings of the crowd. It is very exciting to feel the emotions of those around us. If it wasn't, then a lot of people wouldn't go to ball games, and church on the television would be as satisfying as kneeling down next to someone who has profound faith. But it isn't. Being near someone who has a powerful sense of God's presence is as catching as the excitement of a close game.

The following week's session went very differently:

Jane: I am excited to talk with you!

Therapist: You noticed how your feelings changed when others were in the room with you didn't you?

Jane: Not only that, I saw clearly that when Jack or Sandy was in the room, I felt really anxious. More than that, I noticed that when Allan and Carol came into my office I felt really calm and especially confident. Isn't that something?

Therapist: That is amazing. You are amazing. You took the task very seriously and got even more from it than I had hoped. You did really well. Let me ask you something though. Did either Jack or Sandy actually display any anxiety, or were they not displaying anything in particular.

Jane: No, that is what is so crazy about this.

Therapist: Actually, that is to be expected. If they had shown their emotions overtly, you may not have picked them up. It is when someone is feeling them but not showing or displaying them overtly that others tend to pick up their feelings the most.

Jane: You mean that is partially how come I have been picking up their feelings?

Therapist: Yes, and it is how emotions are more easily passed between people. No one really knows how this actually happens. Some say it is the actual feelings of the person that are passed to the other person. Some claim the two people are harmonizing like harmonizing your voice with a tuning fork, or how a guitar string begins to vibrate when it comes into contact with a music note. Yet, that explanation doesn't really answer all the questions and the truth is that no one really knows right now which it is or how it happens. All we really know is that it does occur and that it can be used for your benefit. It also appears that the person not feeling their feeling and broadcasting it to others isn't actually impacted by those emotions themselves.

Jane: So how do I begin to keep myself safe from their feelings?

Therapist: Well there is a three part sequence to this. First, you have to recognize that you can feel the feelings of others. Second, it is best if you then discover how to let them go when you do notice them. Third, you can then learn how to keep yourself safe, and you just may learn something else at that point.

Jane: Ok, how do I let others' feelings go? I have tried getting up and walking around and even though it helps a little, it doesn't really get rid of them. Actually, the only things that have seemed to help before are going to sleep or encountering some other strong feelings.

Therapist: Wow, you noticed all of that this past week?

Jane: Yes, and I also began to notice how I felt when I was reading a book, or watching a movie. Strong feelings that came from either help me to let go of what others had given me.

Therapist: You are amazing. Most folks wouldn't notice that. They would just want the feelings to stop, and they would be angry, frustrated, or scared to discover anything. They would just be aware of what they didn't want to be aware of. You, however, are willing to learn and to discover what you can know. I like that.

Jane: I don't know that I deserve much praise. I am motivated because I hate feeling this way. I want to be able to have more control over my feelings. I never knew that I was feeling what others felt. I thought it was all just me.

Therapist: While there are a number of ways to let emotions go that you picked up, one way is very simple. Imagine the emotion just flowing out of your body through your hand out into the air, or through your foot into the ground. Your imagination is powerful in this regard and can help you to do it. Sometimes that will be all it takes. Let's practice it.

Jane: What do you mean; I am not feeling anxious right now.

Therapist: That is right, and you can remember a time that you were, can you not?

Jane: Yes.

Therapist: Go ahead and feel those feelings like when you were so anxious that you were almost throwing up. Take your time and remember them. That is right. Now, begin to imagine those feelings going out through your foot into the floor. When you have let go of all those feelings then come on back here and we can talk about it.

Jane: (Excited) it was easy. But wait, I conjured those feelings up by remembering them. Isn't it going to be different when I am in the moment and with someone else?

Therapist: Yes and no. You are very smart to realize these differences. One difference between doing it in the moment when people are around and now is that in the past you were also afraid they would see that you were anxious and look down on you or make fun of you. Actually, it is physically the same either time but much more difficult when also worrying about what someone else thinks.

Jane: Ok, so what are the other ways?

Therapist: I will tell them to you but you will not likely remember them. A second way is to begin to notice whatever feeling that you are feeling. Like right now, are you more curious or frustrated that I said you will never remember them?

Jane: Um, maybe a little frustrated, but I am curious as well.

Therapist: Ok, notice the frustration, and then also notice the room. That is right. Notice everything in the room, including the walls, what is on the walls, and the sounds outside of the building, as well as your curiosity and your desire to learn how to do this, and notice the clock, and the rug on the floor, as well as my voice, and now how are you feeling?

Jane: (Pause) Well that is odd; the frustration is so small that it isn't a problem. (Quizzical look on her face)

Therapist: It happens because when you were aware of the frustration it filled your scope of awareness in the foreground. When you shifted to allowing yourself to be aware of everything around you and kept adding things in, the frustration began to be pushed to the background and then further and further back. It is a way that works pretty well.

Jane: (Sitting silently waiting with a look that says "Please say more")

Therapist: Ok. There is a variation where you can notice the feeling and then notice other things, just like in what you just learned, and then you can intentionally let go of the unwanted emotion. Or, you can intentionally go after feeling a different emotion like curiosity, joy of mastery, or the joy of learning another way to let emotions go that are not helping in the moment.

Jane: (Still sitting silently and waiting)

Therapist: Ok, here is another way, but this is all for today. You can also, ask your unconscious mind how come you are feeling what you are feeling and appreciate that your unconscious mind has had a particular reason to give you that feeling. It may be that in the case of anxiousness that your unconscious mind wanted you to look outside of yourself instead of finding fault and having self- blame. By becoming a detective and appreciating your unconscious mind you will feel better and also perhaps discover some things that are very helpful to you. Often, when we shift to noticing what is going on with others, we can be more helpful both to them and to ourselves by avoiding their feelings. Then when the anxiety is ours, we can overcome it by being helpful and attentive to the other person.

Commentary

This example of Jane being taught by her therapist about anxiety is only one way of teaching it.   Usually, this teaching occurs only when someone comes in with complaints about anxiety. First, I would help them to understand that they really have the strength of intuitive ability which is the reason for the anxiety in the first place. It is simply true that anxiety tends to make the person very intuitive. They sometimes know things and they don't know how they know them, but they do. Ignoring their intuition keeps the smoke detector going off. It is one reason that coming off anti-anxiety drugs returns the person to the hearing the smoke detector going off. When they begin to realize that they are not damaged but instead have a gift, and then find some verification for that, they can then hear some other positive things about themselves. Since this book is more about feeling others feelings and keeping ourselves safe from those feelings, it didn't make sense to divert to the topic of how anxiety also is a positive before illustrating the other. However, usually, I would address that first. Many people have a great deal of difficulty believing that they have a gift instead of a disability.

While Jane's strength has been treated as positive, it can be seen even more positively than that. Jane's problem pointed to her strength just as every problem that you have had is in part because of strengths that you don't know that you have. Since you didn't know, you have used another tool that may not have been as useful for the task. Your problem points to what isn't recognized as strength, if you are willing to see it. Hopefully, this concept will become clearer as we go on.

I suspect part of the reason is that in our culture we have been conditioned to think of problems as only deficiencies, disabilities, and a whole damaged mentality that blames rather than appreciates. However, if we think of something being hurtful, or unpleasant as being our body's way of getting our attention so that we do something different, then we end up with a completely different set of beliefs about ourselves and about the world.

I have helped many folks be in an entirely different place about their anxiety. It is absolutely wonderful to help someone move from thinking of himself/herself as damaged and disabled to gifted and capable. Making the shift does require making a shift in how we understand illness, ourselves, and our culture which says anxiety is only a bad thing that needs medication to deal with it.

The real truth is that while one way that anxiety manifests itself is that others begin to be anxious in our presence, there are a couple of other ways that anxiety happens. The first is when we have developed a self- defeating habit of looking inside of ourselves for the problem when it may well be out-side of us. One of the things I often tell people is that anxiety is like your unconscious tapping you on the shoulder reminding you that the issue that is a problem is out there, and looking for flaws inside of yourself is a guarantee to find flaws. If anyone who is relatively bright focuses on themselves with the question of what did I do wrong or what is wrong with me, they can come up with answers that would result in feeling worse than before.

When folks are anxious they have done such damage to their intuition that they will often need to heal it before it will work well. Consider that by ignoring a person's intuition for extended periods of time would have them not trusting themselves. The only way that any of us keep our intuition working well is to check it out all the time. When we do that our anxiety goes down or disappears and we can feel good about ourselves.

The way that anxiety would alert us would be like in the following sccnc:

You are walking down a hallway when you notice someone whom you know. You say hello to them, only to have them completely ignore your greeting and continue walking staring completely past you. If at the time you feel hurt and/or angry, and then you begin to wonder what could she be angry with me about? What could I have done that she would be so angry with me? Did someone tell her that I commented negatively on her dress last week? I didn't mean it in a bad way, if someone told her that I was being critical of her, I wasn't, but I don't know how to tell her that I wasn't. Did she secretly not like me because of my family? Could it be that I am not cool enough for her?

Ultimately, without asking your friend how come she didn't respond to you, you won't know. In that case, if the self-blame is allowed to continue then it could go on forever. However, another way of dealing with the same scenario would be to recognize that the anxiety may be telling you that there is something going on with your friend and to go talk to her. If you do and she tells you that a close relative is in the hospital in critical care, you would know that your intuition was working just fine. And again you would recognize that you have a gift that you hadn't yet recognized very well. I go into detail about the above way of dealing with anxiety in the book titled, <u>Spiritual Healing of Anxiety and Panic Disorder</u>.

CHAPTER 4

THE PROBLEM OF TOXIC EMOTIONS

*"Fairy Tales are more than true; not because
they tell us that dragons exist, but because
they tell us that dragons can be beaten."*

G. K. Chesterton

*"We teach teenagers and prostitutes to have
safe sex, yet we don't teach therapists how
to stay safe from toxic emotions."*

Carl Whitaker, M. D.

The above quote was told to me by people who knew Carl Whitaker. They told me when I was in graduate school when he was a local legend for the outrageous, yet genius thoughts he uttered. While he was only here in Louisville for a short time, he made a major impact. Some folks said he was brilliant, while others found fault and dismissed his work claiming he was schizophrenic.

I always suspected that their dislike was because what he said rocked the boat so much. In spite of how brilliant Carl Whitaker's statement was, no one ever taught us how to really stay safe from toxic emotions. It became something like the emperor without any clothes. No wonder Whitaker was treated as schizophrenic since his comment was treated the same way that the sometimes brilliant comments of schizophrenics are treated inside the family.

In the professional family of psychotherapy no one was admitting that they didn't know how to stay safe, although everyone was assumed to know, especially anyone who had been practicing for a while. In prison where I worked for a very long time, seasoned employees would assure you that they knew how to stay safe from inmates' emotions. They didn't seem to know how to do this anymore than a rebellious teenager who says, "It doesn't bother me." Like the teenager, they wanted to appear to not allow hurtful or emotional things people dealt with to get to them, but these things did get to them. If you had asked me then, I too would have said, I knew how to do it. Then I probably would have admitted that I didn't know how in the moment to let go but had figured out how to let go of them later easily. While my way was more sophisticated than the teenager's, it still didn't protect in the moment. It simply got rid of the toxic emotions that others gave you. At that time in my career, I didn't believe it was possible to remain safe from other's toxic emotions. I thought the best anyone could do was to let them go later when they realized that they were feeling someone else's feelings.

I would have loved to have known how to protect myself from toxic emotions at the time because I was exposed to them every day. I worked in a prison, and the truth is that being exposed to the toxic emotions of prisoners whose life style and addictions cause them to be emotionally volatile is part of the reason corrections employees have a short life span and are granted hazardous duty pay for their service. When I last looked it up, the average life span of a correctional officer was 59 & ½. That is in spite of the fact that most professionals wouldn't even acknowledge that we pick up others emotions. Corrections employees are given Hazardous duty pay for the stress that they demonstrated and the powerful bodily effects of the stress. The books didn't address the reason for the stress just that it was worse than that of Police officers. At the time, some people believed the reason the stress was so high was because of the dangerousness of some of the inmates. Some believed it was because of the locked up situation where none of us could get away from the inmates. I wasn't convinced about either of those reasons, in part because some of the inmates who had killed were not that scary and being locked up was only a mindset.

I thought that it was because of the volatility of the inmates emotions, but I didn't know how that impacted people. I believed it did impact people but didn't know how. I did know that people were altered by the emotions around them because this was something I saw on a daily basis. In fact we almost always had a crisis of some sort going on. When a knife was lost and was unaccounted for, the inmates were locked down until the knife was found. When sharp barber scissors were lost, the prison would be locked down until they were found. The inmates would become afraid, and the emotion was sometimes so thick that you could almost slice it with your hand. When an inmate would die or escape, it was an emotional roller coaster. While we were exposed to all sorts of emotions regularly, imagine that just talking with inmates meant that you were exposed to their guilt, remorse, anger, fear, and shame all the time, not just when there were crises going on in the institution. In prison, at least the inmates were not likely to have knives or other dangerous objects on them most of the time.

This mattered a lot to me because I was working in a prison at the time. I was the chief chaplain at the women's prison where I offered both religious leadership and therapy, so I was concerned with both the staff and the inmates. We were all exposed to massive amounts of emotion. For over 18 of the 20 plus years that I worked in the prison I also taught at the Louisville Theological Seminary. I taught practical clinical aspects of therapy. So I was paying attention in a practical way to things like emotions both from a personal perspective as well as a professional one. I am the type of person who keeps working on a problem until I have a way to address it. Actually, it is the unique blend of having worked in a prison while teaching counseling techniques and learning about hypnosis at the same time that has allowed me to understand a way to help. It allowed me to put many of the pieces of the puzzle together at the same time. As the findings of neuroscience have progressed along with my understanding of hypnotic trance, ultimately I was able to answer the question and formulate ways that we can keep ourselves safe.

The worst truth is that all of us are exposed to the emotions of others and we are routinely impacted by them whether we acknowledge them or not. Others' emotions impact us more than viruses or fads because we can at least make a decision about whether we choose to allow a fad to have any impact on our behavior. Viruses tend to run their course in a prescribed time, and antibiotics can help bacterial infections. However, the emotions of others often alter how we feel even though we may or may not even be aware of when it happened, or that it happened, or how it happened. The usual scenario is when we have absorbed another person's emotions we tend to believe they are ours, so we treat them and ourselves that way. Once we have treated them as ours it doesn't even occur that we picked them up from someone else. It is my intention to address how to stay safe and how to notice when you have picked up someone else's emotions. Actually, I intend to do a lot more than that but let's start there because the problem is much broader than is implied by therapists and clients. Besides, it is actually a natural extension of how I have taught people to deal with emotions for years. Emotions like sexuality, anger, and fear that are expressed in our presence tend to require a little more finesse than other feelings. For example, just mentioning that someone is emitting sexual feelings in your presence is not going to win friends or influence in any good way. There are a lot of better ways of dealing with this problem, which I will address along with many other things related to emotions and dealing with them.

In almost every situation where more than one person is communicating with another, emotions are being passed. When these emotions are not recognized properly, the result is misunderstandings, blaming, people fighting, eruptions of anger, and many other negative effects. This happens in almost every situation where more than one person is communicating with another. That means that some emotions of lust, greed, fear, and shame are passed just as easily as anger. And they are. Each emotion that is passed without the conscious knowledge of the person receiving the emotion creates a specific problem. While this book will deal with many of them it isn't meant to be so comprehensive. Once you begin to understand some basics, then you can allow your unconscious and your conscious minds to expand the concepts to a variety of feelings and situations. The purpose of this book is to offer real tools to keep you safe and to influence others in positive ways.

This problem has plagued me since I first heard Whitaker's comment. I knew he was right and was frustrated that no one ever taught how to stay safe. Oh, I suspect that some found their own way but they didn't seem to be able to communicate it to anyone else. I asked a lot of people and they all said similar things, like that of course they learned how to, but they never said how, and I saw signs in their behavior that they hadn't really learned how to stay safe, even if they told themselves they had. I thought of it as a problem.

If we think of this as a problem that is masking strengths that we don't know we have then we are in for a whole storehouse of new and exciting discoveries. What if that is true and as a result you discover that not only do you have strengths that you didn't know you have, but that you can also develop them now that you realize what and where they are? Wouldn't that be an incredible journey? I suspect that this radical way of looking at problems just may be that powerful.

For instance, there are many neuroscience folks who claim that all mental health problems are the result of dissociation. That means that all mental health problems are the result of trance since trance is dissociation. You would be surprised at how many respected therapists, physicians, and international researchers recognize this truth. The reason for this comes from the definition of trance, which is dissociation. Just as all those times you were fully present and fully aware of your strengths were trance states, so were all those times you were preoccupied by some feeling of shame, embarrassment, or fear while you were trying to do something else. The second way would be characterized as a negative trance, since it limits your options. The way it tends to work is that the negative trance blocks a person from recognizing their strengths and so they keep on repeating some behavior that was designed to help but doesn't. However, since the person doesn't see their options, strengths, and abilities because the negative trance limits what is seen, they repeat their behavior over and over. Actually, this is good news because if all mental health problems are the result of trance then all people have the ability to go deeply into trance and not just in ways that block our progress and block us from recognizing our strengths. This also means that we can go into positive trances where we not only are aware of strengths but also of abilities that we didn't even know were possible. If the negative limiting trances that come about because of fear, shame, anger, and embarrassment are altered so that we can accept our fear, anger etc., and transform it into strength through being in a positive trance, that would be pretty wonderful. This is not only the case but also only one of the reasons for this book.

CHAPTER 5

WE LEARN THE MOST PROFOUND LESSONS THROUGH EXPERIENCES

*"Every man's life, (or woman's) is a
fairy tale written by God's fingers. "*

Hans Christian Anderson

The most profound lessons and the ones that stick with us the most powerfully are experiences we have that either ratify some aspect of life we believe in deeply or that drastically change how we think. Perhaps the next best thing to being there is to experience a story that tells us and talks to us on multiple levels. I have always appreciated books that speak on more than one level, and it has become a goal of mine to do this and experience this as often as possible. It is easier if you know that you are going to be offered more than one message so that you can appreciate them. Whether you ever see the dual messages I planned, your unconscious will be willing to see the ones that are the best for you. For example, recently I saw a movie that had 8 to 10 different meanings in it. I easily counted 8 and suspected if I watched it again there would have been at least 10. Did the director mean for all those to be there? It doesn't matter because the benefit of the multiple meanings is experienced either way. If I create from a place of trance and offer more than 2 messages it is very likely that there will be far more than that, because in a trance we can speak on more than one level and do so all the time. It is the reason that you can understand things on more than one level at a time as well. It is also the way that advertisements can have such a power-ful effect because they often are speaking on an implied message level, to alter your feelings so that you would be more likely to buy. It wouldn't work if we were not able to notice and respond to the dual and implied messages in advertisements. Ideally, the implied message would have evoked a negative trance where you accepted as fact that if you purchased the product your life would be better. It would help if it could have invited you to be in a negative trance where you were not recognizing all your strengths.

Yet, in a positive trance we are going to communicate and un-derstand far more than we are even meant to because that is how it works. Who we are comes out through our actions. Besides, if we are willing to look for the multiple messages it is also about our willingness to see and hear multiple messages. When we are feeling good about ourselves we are more likely to be in a positive trance and much more aware of our strengths.

Some friends of mine bragged about how wonderful Jim the Bartender was at the Beach Bar on Hilton Head Island. They have a timeshare at the Marriott where the Bar is situated between the Marriott and the Ocean on the beach. They talked about how won-derful he was and how he made people feel good by how he treat-ed them. They raved about this guy and while they spoke about how wonderful and creative his drinks were they were really im-pressed with him as a person. Since they know that I sometimes go to Hilton Head, nothing would do but for me to experience the beach bar and Jim the Bartender. Months went by and at one point I was on the Island with nothing to do since my wife was not feeling well, and so I took a bike ride and was coming back toward where we were staying when I realized that I was close to the beach bar. And so I went there, parked my bike on the beach, leaned it against something near the bar and went in. I was amazed. Jim wasn't beaming from ear to ear but you felt good in his presence, especially when he spoke to you. I saw a small family come into the bar area and in less than a minute Jim had them all smiling, even though he hadn't served them anything, he hadn't told them jokes, and he wasn't just bantering with them. I was beginning to get intrigued. In another minute he was talking to a man across the oval shaped bar from me and suddenly the man was beaming. Then next to me sitting on a bar stool were another two men, who Jim turned to and they were also impacted by his Charisma. While I sipped my beer marveling at how he did it, I was stumped. How could he have had that much impact on someone without really saying anything much to them? While Jim was attractive it wasn't his flirting ability, nor was he making jokes or even being overtly happy. He wasn't beaming, but you would begin to feel better being in his presence. How was or could this happen, I kept asking myself. If I had not seen it then I probably wouldn't have believed it. When my friends told me I was skeptical at the least, but willing to set aside my doubts enough to see for myself. So now that I had experienced it, how could I figure out what it was that he was doing to have that type of an impact.

After the experience with Jim the Bartender, I remembered a waitress who had had the same or similar effect on people. She had been my favorite waitress in a small restaurant my family and I often frequented. I remembered her walking up to people and in less than a minute they were all happy. She too was neither beaming nor telling jokes. She was efficient, never needed to write anything down, and always got the order right, but that wasn't the reason. She made you feel like you were special just by how she looked at you. It was an uncanny ability and it seemed to be something that she just did naturally. Actually, she was so good that men and women were taken by her ability as it had nothing to do with her sex appeal. It was how she treated you and how she looked at you that created the experience. It wasn't possible to see her again as the restaurant had changed hands and she had moved on, but at least I knew or remembered others who had this ability.

Somehow these two people had done something that could be explained, I just hadn't figured it out yet. It made me begin racking my brain for other times that this same thing had occurred. I remembered when I was the prison chaplain, there were two inmates who did this as well. The first was a woman who came to my attention because of some problems that occurred between her and several male chaplain students, one after another over a two year period. This was something that almost never happened before, then one after another five of my male students all complained that they couldn't be a chaplain with her. They all said the same thing, that they found her way too sexy and couldn't be her minister because they didn't trust their reactions with her. When the first man said it, I figured he was just being very smart as she must have reminded him of someone he knew. So I told him it was just to be expected and I praised him for his wisdom and self-knowledge. When the second and third male students said the same thing about finding her too sexy I began to be suspicious. Was she saying or doing something that caused this? She had never been inappropriate with me or around me; however, she had already come to my attention because a teacher in the school had called me to discourage my encouraging her to get a GED.

The teachers all knew how much I tended to encourage the women to get as much education as possible. I had regularly talked with teachers to get insight so that I could help women get more education and so it was odd that they were telling me not to encourage her. They would often tell me things like how bright a student was, or how gifted someone was, so it wasn't at all strange for the teacher to call and talk with me about a student. This time, however, the teacher said, "Chaplain, please don't frustrate either Rachel or us. She just doesn't have enough gray matter. Her intelligence level is so low we won't be able to get her even an 8th grade certificat." I was stunned. The teachers never said anything like that, and they were being serious. Assigning other female students to work with Rachel, I went on and kept the teachers words and pondered what in the world it meant and what the basis of the student's attractions might be. Surely, the basis wasn't that Rachel wasn't as bright. And while Rachel had a relatively pretty face, she was no beauty. There were women in the prison who were absolutely gorgeous, and those women never had any problem and neither did the students working with them. When the next semester two more male students both said the same thing the previous 3 had said, I decided to do more investigation.

Rachel hadn't had any trouble with staff, and she was popular among the inmates, so what could it have been, I kept asking myself. One day Rachel came to the Chapel and I asked her if I could film her for a few minutes. She had no problem being filmed, so while I spoke with her I filmed her responses.

After watching the brief film several times and never getting any closer to how it was that she could have any effect on the men, I turned off the sound and watched a couple of more times. Eureka! It became clear what was going on. Rachel looked at you like you are amazing. She had developed a self-preservation tool to keep safe. When she looked at you it was with such admiration and appreciation that those five men had all felt sexual feelings toward her. For them being looked at as if they were that amazing was so sexy that they couldn't trust themselves. For Rachel her look was more like that of a puppy who wants to be liked and so it is so excited to see you.

At least those students were all smart enough to not get into trouble with someone who they found that attractive, because another inmate had gotten 3 staff members fired because they all fell in love with her. The Warden wanted to know what was happening so we could make changes and help the staff be more protected. The Warden asked me to investigate what was going on. I went to talk with Becky. She was very happy to talk with me, and even to talk about whatever I wanted as she was willing to help. Now, the most flattering thing that I can say about Becky was that she had pretty hands. Childhood had pockmarked her face, which wasn't all that attractive to begin with, and she didn't have any outgoing ability or even the looks that Rachel had. What on earth could it have been that caused her to be so appealing that three officers had been willing to lose their jobs over falling in love with her. Actually, all three men had positions of responsibility and were not just plain line staff or even people who had been just hired in. These were seasoned officers who should have known how to stay safe. They hadn't, and they had lost their careers, pensions, and probably their self-respect. They knew that by falling in love with an inmate in the prison where they worked there would be consequences. Losing a pension, career, and job, didn't bring any caution. They were head over heels in love.

As we talked, I realized that Becky was willing to talk to you like you were amazing. In her presence you might begin to feel 10 feet tall, and sought after like a rock star. It wasn't anything sexual, it was emotional. It was how she had learned to be safe. She was horribly abused as a child, had been abused by her husband, and had developed an approach, over time, that seemed to slow down the abuse. She would talk to you as if you were amazing. It wasn't that she was complimentary, but it was how she spoke. At least that was how I explained it for a long time. Her words did have a powerful effect. Not only had she gotten three men fired, but she was in prison for talking a neighbor into killing her husband for her. Not long after my talking with her she began writing to men on the outside and found one who fell in love with her and married her.

Back then I hadn't known about mirror neurons or the possibility of someone passing feelings to another person. It wasn't something that anyone believed and, even more, it wasn't something that was going to answer anything, or so I thought back then. Today, I would explain Becky's attraction not only as being her words, mannerisms, and body language; I would suggest that Becky was also sending off an emotional message that implied you were very impressive. This was also something that Rachel had been doing, but I didn't have the knowledge of it being possible back when I was learning about her and the whole experience.

The truth is there are politicians and actors who have that same sort of charisma. You have probably been in the presence of folks who have that sort of ability. In fact, I would almost guarantee that you have, the only question is whether you noticed it or not. At the prison we had celebrities who often came there with various prison groups, ministry teams, or on their own. There were attractive folks and ones who were absolutely beautiful or handsome. Their charisma isn't what I am talking about. There is a mystique that goes with being famous that causes people to want to see, hear, and talk with famous people, but that isn't at all what is going on.

There are folks who when they turn on the charm it is suddenly so powerful that you feel noticed, singled out, or spoken to personally even in the midst of a crowd. Those folks can often get things done, and their charisma doesn't come through very well on the TV. Yes, they are good communicators. Yes, they can persuade folks well, but it isn't the same thing.

You have felt it with some folks. You may even have it yourself. So, what is it?

CHAPTER 6

HOW THIS SYSTEM WORKS

*"If you want your children to be intelligent, read
them fairy tales. If you want them to be more
intelligent then read them more fairy tales. "*

Albert Einstein

Jane: So how does it work?

Therapist: You have felt it and you have used it what did you decide is how it might work?

Jane: We…. Well does it work because we can only be aware of so many things at once?

Therapist: That is a good hypothesis, and it may be as good of hypotheses as what I am going to give you. In fact, yours may have some very powerful merit.

Jane: You mean my guess might be right?

Therapist: It might not only be right…there are some physical reasons that your guess might be the reason. It seems that if you have pain in one area and then cause pain to another area or overload the nerves carrying the sensory information, that it will stop sending the pain message. This is the reason that during a movie a person in pain may just forget all about the pain and actually only later realize that the pain was gone during the movie.

Jane: Wow!

Therapist: The theory I have been operating from uses trance as the focal point. In effect, it says that when you are paying attention to several things at once you will be in a trance. While you are maintaining your trance by remaining aware of certain feelings that you are not showing to others, you are actually projecting those emotions to others. It tends to protect you from emotions that they are or might be sending toward you. It may be that it works because of the same or similar way that pain is blocked, but I have thought it was because of the positive nature of the expanded trance being more powerful than a negative trance through which someone would be sending their criticism, fear, hurt or anger.

Jane: So you mean that all I have to do is to feel some feeling that I don't show or attempt to not show, and I can then be more protected from how others are feeling?

Therapist: That is certainly one way, and it would especially work if that feeling was something that you wanted to share with the person you were talking with. It probably also needs to be some positive feeling and not one of fear, anger, shame or embarrassment.

Jane: What if I don't want to share a sense of confidence, mastery, or joy with the person who I want to stay safe from?

Therapist: Well you could feel fear, and not show it so that was what was projected. But it might just attract folks who would want to take advantage of you. Not wanting to send any positive feelings toward others who might just be sloshing their toxic feelings toward you probably wouldn't work very well. In effect, your desire to get even, not give something positive or to keep from them might put you at more risk.

Jane: Great, so now I have to give to the people who are hurting me, sometimes every day.

Therapist: I didn't say that, but somehow you heard that. I guess I wasn't clear. Your wanting to keep them from improving, changing or becoming better might not only not help them to stop being quite so toxic in their interactions it might make it worse. Your anger puts you a little at risk. That is all.

Jane: You are saying that I have to deal with my own anger and not get even in some way with this?

Therapist: In so many words, yes. This is so because your anger hurts you and makes you more vulnerable in ways that the next technique that I can teach you may or may not help with because your anger is yours. It is a reflection of your beliefs, hurts, etc. Someone said that holding anger toward someone else is like taking poison and waiting for the other person to get sick. It isn't helpful to us.

Jane: But that isn't fair! They hurt me and yet I still have to work to deal with what they did and what they said. They seem to get off Scott free.

Therapist: That again isn't really the way it works. The truth is there is no one who ever gets away with anything. There are always consequences. You may not see the effects of their bad behavior, but they are there. It is one of the most shocking things truths that I discovered while working in prison...no one ever gets away with anything. Yes, of course people get away with crime, but they don't get away with any form of hurting others because the consequences always impact them. However, your feelings are yours. Someone else's feeling is theirs. If you are feeling a certain feeling, even if that was initiated by someone else, once you have it then it is yours.

Jane: So what are these other techniques?

Therapist: First is to take responsibility for our feelings, and even to learn from them and to use the knowledge about us so that we are less vulnerable to folks doing similar things. This is more difficult than it seems. Second is to recognize that I am only vulnerable because I am not recognizing something good about me to even be vulnerable.

Jane: What. That doesn't make sense.

Therapist: Right next to any fear that I have is a strength that I am not recognizing or else it wouldn't be a fear. General fears don't tend to plague a person. It is only fears that are attached to events we have experienced or are afraid to experience because of some near miss or because of special circumstances. As soon as you are aware of your strengths then the fear would more naturally simply fall back into obscurity, unless it would be something that anyone would be afraid of, like an angry mountain lion, tiger, or alligator.

Jane: You mean fears like of flying, driving, having someone angry with us are all because we don't see or pay attention to strengths that we have?

Therapist: That is right. You have it exactly. So as long as someone is willing to learn from any fear that they have by looking at the strength they have not been paying attention to, then they can also easily learn a new technique to be safe around toxic emotions. If we are willing to learn from our fear it is then a simple enough matter to imagine a plastic or Plexiglas barrier around us that protects us. The imagination of the Plexiglas shield invites us to be in a positive trance. It is almost impossible to imagine the shield while doing other things and not be in a trance, and since you are doing this to protect yourself it is very likely that it would be a positive trance. It is a way to be safe. Ultimately, using that approach for a short period of time would work fine. However, it implies that you need protection. Another way would involve you holding an emotion in your mind that protects you by you broadcasting that emotion. This technique implies that you are not only ok but in charge of even more than just yourself.

Jane: You keep talking about the positive trance what is the difference between that and a negative trance or no trance?

Therapist: A good way to describe a positive trance is when you are doing two or more things at a time while being aware of everything around you and inside of you. Some folks would liken it to a mindful state. Yet, it is possible to be mindful and not be in a positive trance where you are also aware of your strengths, weaknesses, and are accepting of them. Does that make sense?

Jane: I think so… Well what is the difference between a positive trance and a mindful state?

Therapist: None in some instances. However, some folks understand being mindful as being aware of what is going on around of a person, being accepting of those things that are happening, and being accepting of the self as well. I think of the positive trance as being a state of mind that is hyperaware of what is going on around nearby but also nonjudgmentally accepting it from a positive emotional place where you are also very aware of your strengths, options, abilities, as well as even your weaknesses that you are accepting of because of your awareness of the strengths. From my perspective, a positive trance would be a mindful state, but it isn't necessarily true that all mindful states would be inviting a person to be in a positive trance. It is the altered state of consciousness that occurs from being in a trance where things seem to just happen without being directed that might make the difference. I am not sure. Your question is an excellent one.

Jane: So, if I allow myself to be more fully aware of everything around me while shifting my senses so that I am hyperaware and almost passively accepting the awareness that is occurring while being aware of my strengths at the same time, I would be in a positive trance?

Therapist: Yes! How about practicing it right now? Are you willing? If so, keep your head still and your eyes still and expand your awareness of everything in the room, allowing yourself to become more and more aware of all your strengths as simply factual, then begin to acknowledge and notice how your consciousness changes.

Notice how the things you are aware of simply changes and your ability to sense what is going on also increases. That is right just allow that ability and awareness to be there while you enjoy the different perspective and heightened awareness.

Jane: You went there with me, didn't you?

Therapist: Yes, how did you know?

Jane: Your voice changed, and you didn't blink. You stared right at me and didn't blink, maybe ever. How does that help?

Therapist: It helps me because that has been a way for me to do it. Blinking lowers the intensity of what I am aware of and so I intentionally blink less, while I am going there deeply with you. I stay as complexly connected to you and whatever is going on in the room as possible, so I blink very little. It probably has very little to do with it but it seems to help when I am doing it with someone else. When I do it myself for me I don't really need to do that in the same way. It is really the intensity that makes the difference.

Jane: So, what about the negative trance?

Therapist: The negative trance occurs when a person is very aware of their fear, hurt, or anger. Actually, any variation of fear, embarrassment, shame, hurt, anger, jealousy, envy, or even lust would or could be the source of the negative trance. A person who is aware of say jealousy, and trying not to show it or even allow it to be important to them would be in a negative trance. They would not be as aware of their strengths, and mostly only aware of their weaknesses. The major difference would be that the person didn't want or believe it was right to be hurt, angry, jealous, or lustful, and was trying not to be it. Their attempt to not be doing what they were doing would induce a negative trance where they would be screening out things instead of including them in. Their doing two things at a time and not accepting the feelings that they were having at the time would very likely alter their thinking, and then they would be seeing things mostly from a negative trance. As a result, they would likely make bad decisions. Often, those decisions become worse even after studying a lot about what to do.

Jane: What about not being in a trance state? How would that alter the occasion? We can't be in a trance state all the time, or are we?

Therapist: No, we are not in a trance all the time, or if we are then what we call a normal state is the conglomeration of past trances and programmed positives and negatives from all those other experiences. I don't really think that has anything to do with it. However, when a person is in a normal state they are probably more vulnerable to emotions that others might be projecting or sloshing around.

Jane: So, the only way we are more protected is when we are in a positive trance?

Therapist: That is how I see it. In fact, I suspect that being in a negative trance almost invites someone who is also in a negative trance to spill some of their feelings onto us. However, it is almost impossible to go from a negative trance to a neutral or no trance. That is what happens when someone is feeling fear and wants to not feel it. Trying not to feel the fear simply won't work. You can easily go from a negative trance to a positive one but not to a neutral one. And you can also easily go from a positive trance to no trance.

Jane: You mean like when my husband or I are feeling bad, or in a bad mood, and soon both of us are in a bad mood.

Therapist: Yes. Absolutely!

Jane: You mean that when my husband comes home and is in a bad mood, if I went into a positive trance I could avoid the negative one and maybe even alter his bad mood?

Therapist: You know, that is right. Not many folks get it that fast, and most don't make that connection with arguments. They don't see that the negative trance they or their partner was in can be easily picked up by the other one and played back. What is especially impressive is that you recognize that if you go into a positive trance it is going to at least keep you safe, and it might do even more than that and alter his negative one.

Jane: Thanks. Now I have another question for you, because you said you would tell me other techniques and you only told me about a couple.

Therapist: Your memory is amazing. You are right, I only told you how to use the Plexiglas shield. These techniques come from NLP(Neural Linguistic Programing) and span the gauntlet of introducing things like Plexiglas shields, being circled in white light, or wearing a protective cloak, suit of armor, or bullet proof vest. You can use anything that takes imagination and you have some positive connection to. One man I know puts on a bear suit of love that allows him to ward off any negativity, criticism, or hurtful things and to see those things in a different light. For example, he might interpret an awkward experience with someone as the person's positive attempt at connecting with him. He is amazing. Another woman I know has been able to deal with her family in new ways that allow her to be around them without getting so uptight and hurt that she could hardly stand it.

Jane: So it would work if I imagined myself wearing a protective shawl, wearing a protective coat, or seeing myself circled in gold rows that protect me?

Therapist: You could imagine yourself wearing a golden crown or saint's halo, and be protected by it. It is best to use imagery that is important to you and that you have some positive connection with so that it conveys some positive feeling or sentiment for you. Of course, it isn't the image itself nor even the power of the imagery that does it. It is the two things being done at once that induces a mild dissociation from your perceptions that we call a trance. And it is this creation of trance that protects you. Since you are doing it intentionally it would be a positive trance where you would be more aware of your strengths and abilities as well as fully aware of everything else going on around you.

Commentary

All of the above may seem frivolous. It is meant to be a little bit, because the whole concept is so simple yet powerful that it is difficult to take it too seriously. The people whom I have taught this technique have all liked it, in part because it is something that makes sense as it induces a mild trance that alters normal perception. There is nothing magical about it yet there is everything magical about it because it makes so great of a difference. Some of the people who have learned this have been able to deal with difficult family members, customers, and bosses with a lot of success. Some have become more able to relate with and have calmed down partners who have become defensive or fearful about a personal trigger like money, sex, family, etc.

It is so simple and yet no one in therapy school was teaching it and no one at the women's prison was using it that I knew about when I was there. We all said we knew how to avoid the toxic emotions but none of us really did. We all simply tried to let them go or to tell ourselves that we weren't really ingesting the emotions around us. Everyone at the prison knew these things weren't true, but no one was any more willing to admit this falsity than the therapists were willing to admit they didn't know how to avoid the toxic feelings of others.

If you think about it, this is exactly what Jim the Bartender was doing. Not only was he protecting himself and having a positive influence on people, it also meant a huge difference in his being able to be exposed to so many toxic emotions at the bar over so many years and not be burned out.

Stress doesn't come from the event itself. It comes from our experience of it. If we think of it as being something we can avoid or have an option to cope with it, the event is probably going to have little or no negative effect. In fact, 75% of the people who are exposed to traumatic events don't have negative effects. The 25% who do have trauma from what they experienced felt that they didn't have any options. Not recognizing any options causes a person to feel so powerless that they experience the negative effects of the trauma. Ironically, when people see their options, they not only don't feel the negative stress they actually feel like they have accomplished something, and they have.

I know people who have become able to deal with folks that they had previously avoided. Others who have become able to cope with people socially who give off negativity, hurtful feelings, and horrible criticism, and still remain ok. It is because they can remain ok in their own emotions and avoid the fear, hurt, and anger of the other people that makes the difference.

Another way of thinking about how it works would be with an analogy. Years ago, I taught people to deal with critical folks by being a matador with them. I taught them to hold out a cape that the bull would come after and then to move the cape, just like a matador might. When the bull begins to come at the matador he/she is standing behind the cape. When the bull gets closer the cape is moved to the side, and then when the bull comes close the matador is safe and the bull passes harmlessly.

When we shift from one perception to another we are being like the matador. We are not emotionally where the other person might hurt us. We are somehow beside ourselves standing on our side and being our own friend. We are also being a friend to the one who is so toxic because they often have no idea that they are and also no idea that they are infecting those around them. If we avoid it we are also offering to them a new way of being. It is catching.

If, however, instead of just avoiding the bull, we tag it with some positive emotion, then we are doing the exact opposite of what the bull fighter does in the ring. Matadors tag the bull with long sharp rods and would ultimately kill the bull. What if we did something very different? Imagine a bull fighter that actually, heals, helps and affirms the bull each time that he passes so that after a while the bull doesn't try to hurt the matador because he knows that the matador has treated him well. With each pass you have healed, helped, and nurtured the bull and tagged with a positive affirmation. You then have tamed the bull and haven't fought it in the usual sense but actually healed it.

There is a form of martial arts that invites you to see through the eyes of your attacker and to become as close as possible. That way you are less likely to become hurt.

A true story that I was told about a man who went to Japan to study Aikido. He studied and practiced Aikido, day in and day out. He wanted to become adept at the use of it, so he worked very hard. He punched, blocked, kicked, and in general learned how to disarm almost any situation. He was very proud of himself. Since he was so accomplished, he wanted to put his new skills to use in some practical fashion. One day while he was on the subway in Japan, a large man got on the train, stumbling, pushing and in general causing a trouble for everyone on board that car. The man was obviously drunk. The new aikido master decided this was the time he would be able to do something. He would use his new skills and stop this man from hurting others. He got up and started toward the drunken man, and felt himself mentally prepare for hand to hand combat. Everyone on board could tell a confrontation was about to happen. Just as the new aikido master got close, a little man stood up between the new aikido master and the drunk. Then the little man said to the drunken man, "Excuse me sir, have you been drinking sake?" The drunk said, "What is it to you?" The little man said, "Oh, it is because every evening my wife and I have sake, and sit in the garden. It is very pleasant. We enjoy it a lot." The drunk sat down and began to cry. He said, "My wife just left me. That is why I drink sake." The old man comforted the drunk and the crisis was averted. The new aikido master realized that he had witnessed a true aikido master at work in the little man. He felt humbled and realized he'd been taught a powerful lesson.

CHAPTER 7

OVERT AND COVERT EMOTIONS

*"Some day you will be old enough to
start reading fairy tales again. "*

C. S. Lewis

We all deal with emotions all the time from others, whether we recognize it or not. Most of the time we do very well, but sometimes we don't. It doesn't matter, unless it matters and has become a problem.

We deal with emotions of others that are overt. When someone is angry, happy, or sad and their face shows it, that means one thing and it is dealt with differently than other emotions that others expose us to. For the most part, we as a culture don't really know what to do if someone is crying and demonstrating that sadness out in public. Some of us may know what to do depending on how close we are to the person but when powerful emotions are presented in front of us we don't really have any roadmaps for how to deal with them. Who hasn't wondered what to say at a funeral when the person in front of you has been sobbing, or began sobbing in your arms? While it is good to know what to do, it is also difficult not to absorb those powerful emotions that are expressed in front of you. It is very difficult to see someone who is grieving and not feel loss, especially if you have lost a loved one. It is very difficult not to feel sadness when we hold someone who is crying so hard that they are shaking uncontrollably. It is also a very loving thing to do to just hold them and allow their emotion to spill out while we are caring about the person and ignoring their grief.

It is reasonably possible when we are the one holding the person in our arms while they are sobbing because it is very clear what is happening, we usually deal with the emotion well. Their emotion and body language is very congruent. What they are saying, feeling and communicating are all the same message. While we may not know what to do with their powerful emotion, most of us can understand it and empathize with it. We are not usually scared of that sort of emotion, at least not in the moment. It is clean and real, and what is seen is also what is felt.

The same is true when we are in the presence of a baby smiling, playing, and being cute. Most of us can feel good, enjoy the moment, and are really ok about the congruence of emotion that the baby is showing and what we are feeling. We trust the messages. It would be similar if a baby was crying. We might not like it, but it wouldn't be something that would bother us beyond being annoying that someone wasn't taking care of addressing what was bothering the baby. The baby's crying wouldn't necessarily be a problem for us. Of course if we had lost a child or there was something in our past that the baby's crying brought up, that would be a different thing but for the most part it wouldn't be an emotional problem for us.

However, anger expressed in front of us repeatedly does have an impact and limits our options for dealing with angry situations in the future. It is simply a fact that being exposed to someone's angry displays of emotion would tend to impact those exposed to it. We would be more prone to either exploding or wilting away from that type of anger.

Culturally we only allow for powerful expressions of emotion such as kissing, hugging for long periods, etc., to be expressed at airports, bus stations, or other similar venues. Emotionally charged kissing would be frowned upon at the grocery, department store, or in a hallway at a college. It would be a little more acceptable at a movie theater, but how come?

People in a panic who are displaying the fear on their face are usually tolerated and seldom cause us a problem. We might find them needing psychiatric help, but we probably wouldn't be personally experiencing their emotions as toxic. It might, at most, be annoying or mildly unsettling but it wouldn't be something that would bother us too much.

However, when we are exposed to emotions that are sending two messages at the same time we are more likely to be distressed, unsettled, or contaminated with the toxic emotion that is expressed.

For instance, when someone is very emotionally expressive of sweetness and niceness, and yet just under the surface we can sense a deeper and more angry, mean, or fearful emotion, then we have a dilemma. We don't know which emotion to pay attention to and which to ignore or pay less attention to. We also have to know what is really being said or which is the more powerful message that is being communicated to us between the two emotions. There are all sorts of messages sent that are conflicting, as well as affirming or correcting what is being communicated overtly. So we really do need to decide how to respond to both messages. Are we going to believe one and ignore the other, or address both? Which is the emotion that we need to deal with and which isn't that important? Which one gives us more difficulty and which ones don't? These are all things that we deal with all the time. So how come mostly none of those emotions give us too much trouble? When we clearly are seeing and sensing the contradictions between what is displayed and what is felt from the person, we usually have ways of coping with those situations, even if they do at times cause us to make not such good decisions. When we want someone to like us, and their words say they do but their actions say they don't, we might have trouble because we want to believe their words even if we deep down are preparing ourselves for the inevitable. But that difficulty is about us really. We don't want to see what we know we see.

We usually deal well enough with emotions that don't just disagree with what is being said, but actually contradict it. Most of us don't really struggle with that. While saying one thing and doing another with our emotions that are clearly displayed to others is something we might smile at or frown upon, it isn't something that gives us too much trouble. For instance, when someone is saying they don't want to buy a car but they are in fact buying a car from us, it isn't something that bothers us much. This is true even when the communication is more confusing like, "I love you but I think we should go out with other people.", where the words are saying one thing but the contradiction is clear. Of course, when we want the person to still be with us we may have more difficulty, but eventually we would see through it and accept that it was over.

What we tend to have difficulty with are emotions that are not acknowledged by the person and or are in contrast to what we see on their face. For instance when someone is deeply depressed but hiding it with enthusiasm, jokes, or an upbeat air, we may feel the depression and not know that it is coming from them but blame ourselves. If we were very sensitive we would likely pick up the depression from them and have to deal with the emotions on our own. Because culturally we don't acknowledge that folks can pass emotions like that, the recipient often blames themselves and wonders if they are crazy. There are a lot of folks spreading a whole host of emotions to others and are oblivious to it.

Typhoid Mary as she was called spread typhoid fever to people while she fixed food for them. She was a cook, who had a rare condition of having typhoid germs that could be passed to others even though she was immune to the germs herself. She spread typhoid fever to a lot of folks, and even when she was told that she was a carrier she kept on infecting others. Some attribute her actions with intention. I suspect she simply didn't believe people who were blaming her for the deaths of many people. She wasn't sick and she didn't believe that she was a carrier. I have a difficult time believing that she intentionally hurt others. Not many folks are really that cold and calculating. When they are, it is so obvious, but common belief attributes to Mary some harmful intent. In my experience, such common beliefs are usually wrong. Besides if you attribute only malevolent intent you have fewer options to stay safe. There would have been other indicators that would have shown if Mary was really intent on hurting others. There are indications that she was in denial of her effect. Being told that you were responsible for the deaths of many people who you liked and cared about would be very difficult to accept, especially when you didn't have a lot of education or even many friends left.

CHAPTER 8

TRADE IN YOUR CODEPENDENCY FOR A STRENGTH

*"Once in a while, right in the middle of an
ordinary life, love gives us a fairy tale. "*

Author Unknown

What is usually mislabeled as Codependency is a state where the person is responding to the mixed messages that are being communicated to them. On the surface the addict says they want to quit, but their actions say something else. The mixed communication causes quite a stir in most folks who love an addict. However, it isn't the actions that are the culprit but the emotion that seems to be emitted at the same time that makes for dealing with the addict more difficult.

If we were to only address the discrepancy between the person's words and their actions we would be at least baffled, buffaloed, or something. It doesn't look as if the person is really interested in changing, or they don't look like they are taking the process seriously.

However, if you were to also examine what emotions they were emitting in people's presence you would find a very different possibility.

Usually what is occurring is that the addict is emitting an emotion, such as a sense of responsibility or fear, and they themselves are not feeling it. Anyone nearby who cares about the addict and is sensitive to picking up feelings will sense the emotions that are being emitted but not felt. Here is an example:

George: My daughter is an addict. She says she wants to quit, but she doesn't, and I am in such a quandary that I don't know what to do about it.

Therapist: Remind me of how you tend to feel in her presence?

George: What are you talking about? I just told you she is an addict and I don't know what to do about it.

Therapist: I heard you. When she is talking to you, how do you feel?

George: Oh, well I feel alright.

Therapist: Yes, I know that you feel alright. The feelings that you experience when you are in her presence are what? They are different from what you feel when you are by yourself or before she walks into the room.

George: Oh, I see. Well, when she comes into the room, I am a little bit anxious, because I don't know how it is going to go. Like Saturday, when she came to talk to me about borrowing money to go out with her friends, it just didn't feel right. I found myself feeling afraid and overly responsible for her and her friends.

Therapist: Yes, that is what I expected.

George: What do you mean?

Therapist: You started to feel the feelings that she wasn't feeling and so you found yourself feeling afraid, and overly responsible. It is what often occurs.

George: So what are you saying?

Therapist: She is not feeling the feelings of being responsible and you are. She also isn't feeling afraid and you started feeling that in her presence. No wonder she doesn't make good decisions. She is able to not feel the feelings that would have helped her to make better decisions.

George: Are you accusing me of something?

Therapist: No, I am acknowledging that often addicts emit emotions that those who care about them tend to feel. What I haven't talked to you about is how you can give them back. That is right, you can literally offer the feelings back to her.

George: Are you pulling my leg?

Therapist: Let me tell you a story. Once when I was seeing a young man who was very depressed, the young man discovered a way that stopped the depression. His solution, however, was to get an adrenalin high. The trouble was that he was getting his high in ways that put him and others at risk. He would get one of his friends to drive his car 60 miles an hour while he rode on the top of it and held on. Sometimes he would surf outside of the car when it was raining. He would hold on to the door and the car, while allowing his feet to hydroplane on the expressway. I started feeling afraid and responsible. I wanted to say something that would get him to think straight, and then it hit me. I was picking up his feelings, and as long as I had them there was no incentive for him to change. So I figured that if I could receive them, I could also give them back. I did, and then he decided to continue getting his adrenalin high but in safe ways. He realized that he was putting his friends and himself at risk. George you can do the same thing. I have taught this to a lot of people since that young man taught it to me.

George: You are serious?

Therapist: I am not only serious; there are plenty of studies that indicate how we actually pick up the feelings of others. It isn't widely known any more than the fact that your brain continues to grow if you think and use it. People used to teach that after a certain age the brain was losing brain cells for the rest of a person's life.

We have known better for a long time now, but there are a lot of people who still believe what they were taught in school. Granted, George, we don't really know how we as humans feel other people's feelings, but we do. Actually, there are some debates about it. Some say it is only a harmony effect that we feel, and some say we feel the feelings that are not felt by the other person. I say it is both.

George: So how do I give them back?

Therapist: That is easy; imagine that you are giving them back. I like to do it with a gesture, while I intentionally go into a shift of consciousness, but I don't know that is necessary. The shift in consciousness I go into is mainly an altering of what I am aware of at the moment. I allow myself to become highly aware of everything around me shifting my focus of awareness from just on the emotions, or just on the person to everything around me and then imagine giving the feelings back.

George: That sounds too easy. This has felt horrible. I have been frustrated, angry, and hurt, and so has my wife. This has caused us a huge amount of problems. She has been going to a co-dependency group. I heard about you having a different way of treating addicts and I thought I would come here.

Therapist: The feelings we have in an addict's presence are predictable. When folks don't know that they are feeling the feelings that would help an addict to change, they get all frustrated, anxious, and fearful, yet they still are not helpful to the addict. What co-dependence groups tend to teach is that a person has to become willing to offer tough love and refuse to help the addict, or to become cold to their feelings. You may be interested in knowing that science doesn't acknowledge co-dependency because the criteria for it are so broad that every man woman and child in the world could be labeled as co-dependent. I think the way I am suggesting is a much more appropriate and reasonable way. If you want to read about co-dependency as a myth, I think the book is 50 myths of psychotherapy. I forget who wrote it, but it is by multiple authors. Not bad reading, even if co-dependency is only a small part of the book.

George: You really are serious.

Therapist: Yes, and when you begin to give your daughter's feelings back you will see options that you haven't seen before. She too will see new options, although she may take a little longer. By the way, she will probably be much more compliant and you two will get along a lot better. Oh, and I advise against telling your wife what I have told you until you have done it and begin to get results. If you even wait for a short while after beginning to get results, she will be intrigued and want to learn it too. If you tell her today, she will think you are as crazy as she will think that I am. This whole concept is challenging her world view, and things that she has believed. It will go better if it happens slowly.

George: (Smiling) I think that just might be fun.

Commentary

Lots of folks have benefited from understanding this concept. They not only stopped feeling so bad about themselves but also began to find ways of impacting the addict in their life.

Scientifically, there is no such thing as co-dependency. The reason it doesn't exist in science is actually a simple one. The reason isn't that people feel powerful things in the presence of addicts but that every human being could qualify for being co-dependent. An illness that everyone has isn't an illness. It is a trait of being human. It is simply a realization of being capable of feeling the feelings of others who are not feeling them.

The people who lead co-dependency groups or teach co-dependency classes simply haven't explored what we are discussing, nor have they paid attention to the science that says co-dependency doesn't exist or how come people have strong feelings in the presence of addicts. The reason that medicine didn't find a cure or the cure I am offering here is that they were looking for illness and dysfunction in the person dealing with the addict. These persons have often acted in less than good ways, but those ways have often kept them safe and helped the addict maintain their addiction.

Using the tools I'm offering not only helps the person involved with the addict; ultimately, it also helps the addict. It offers a way of dealing with addicts that is compassionate and understands them in ways that are healing, not blaming. It is something that I have been teaching people about for some time.

CHAPTER 9

SEXUAL FEELINGS ARE NOT ALWAYS ABOUT SEX, EVEN IF THEY FEEL THAT WAY

"I used to be Snow White, but I drifted. "

Mae West

Sexuality and sexual feelings get expressed in ways that are not easily discussed because of the many different meanings that can be and often are suggested. It can be difficult to discuss how come the way someone dresses or sits is sexually provocative. Talking about it often gets people in trouble and not talking about it often gets people in trouble, so what does a healthy person do?

Because it isn't easily discussed and because we don't tend to acknowledge that emotions can be broadcast, it makes for easy misunderstandings. It also makes dealing with people who are radiating sexual emotions very difficult. We don't really know if it is them or us who is having that much sexual feelings going on and this makes for a confusing situation. So how do you tell if it is them or you? There are times when it is clearly them, but those may not be easy to see without some foreknowledge. It is a very dangerous situation.

For instance, when someone has sexual shame they are trying not to show, they may be sloshing sexual feelings and not be aware of it because they are so focused on how much shame they have. Their attention to their shame would then make them even more oblivious to the fact that they were radiating sexual feelings. It sounds difficult to believe, but that is often what happens, and it is a very difficult double bind for anyone encountering them. While they seem to be sending a message to be sexual with them, because they are not aware of the emotions they are sending they might just be shocked or surprised if someone pointed it out or acted on those messages.

The quickest way to be attacked verbally and or legally would be to comment on the sexual feelings that someone in that situation was giving off. Since they have no conscious awareness of what they are emitting they are not going to take responsibility for what YOU pick up from them. It really has no bearing on the fact that they are the ones expressing and broadcasting the emotions. Any attempt to give them responsibility will be punished.

Just like in other scenarios where the person isn't going to take responsibility for the emotions that they are emitting, it is also true in the case of sexuality. It is one of the ways that people get themselves into a lot of trouble. Perpetrators get into trouble because they respond to these displays of sexuality and either have sex or try to initiate sex. In both cases, the perpetrator is then in trouble. Victims who have no idea they are expressing such emotions to others will deny, defend, and become indignant. It is a real problem. How can you know when what you are picking up on is really an invitation or when it is a cry for help? If it is an invitation, then you would be better off going in the other direction. The reason is that anyone who sloshes sexual feelings and isn't aware of it has enough issues to make being in a relationship difficult, at least until they heal. After they heal, they won't slosh those feelings around. So responding only to the invitation would be foolish on many levels, but helping the person crying out for help also poses danger; it just isn't as foolish as attempting to have a relationship with someone who is incapable of doing it.

To teach people about this concept and how to stay safe, I often begin by explaining the major reasons that people might express sexual emotions. The first reason is to just receive some sort of attention. Lots of folks, male and female, use sex as a means to get attention and affection that they crave. Their inappropriate use of sexuality can be annoying or alluring, but what is displayed, emitted, or portrayed may not be at all what the other person experiences. We all know about some of the reasons that people use sex to receive some sort of affection and attention. One woman at the prison told me that she would often have sex with men just so that they would hold her. She was so starved for affection, that she would have sex just to be touched. She craved any kind of nurture and acknowledgement she could get, and she was that open and honest about it.

Secondly, some folks use sex as a tool for power. Not only through the usual means of getting power with sex, but also through being able to attract and then say no so that they have the upper hand. One woman I counseled had been a victim of that. She was, at first, wooed powerfully so that she started to be interested, and then the guy pulled back and made sure that she knew he was also dating others. It is a common way people bolster their ego at the expense of anyone they date. As soon as they get someone interested in them they widen the field so that they always have someone waiting in the wings. It helps them to feel more powerful and to feel more attractive. Whether people have really thought about it or not, they will understand that one of the primary reasons that folks have affairs is to get even with an abusive or neglectful partner.

Third, people sometimes use sex for expressing revenge. Sometimes the revenge is to the person they were dating or are married to, and the anger they feel is expressed in sex or by having sex. Sometimes it is expressed to people who respond to their come-ons. More than one prostitute has told me about the disdain they had for people who acted holier than thou and yet responded to the sexual stimulus they offered. They were not above exploiting anyone who responded to them. During the years I worked in prison only two or three women came to prison for having AIDS and continuing to have unprotected sex with men. One told me that someone gave it to her and she was going to give AIDS to as many people as she could. She was so angry and unapologetic that she told this to me, a chaplain. Usually folks who are that angry are interested in hiding it from ministers. She wasn't. She did know that I knew she had been arrested for intentionally spreading AIDS. I never knew whether it was partially an act or whether it was because she was really that angry. As I remember it, I couldn't feel the anger from her, only fear. So was she only acting upon revenge, or was she displaying her fears because of her inadequacies?

Fourth, it isn't as widely known that some folks use sex to display their inadequacies, or to hide them. In the prison I never met a woman who had been a prostitute that hadn't been sexually abused or molested in one fashion or another. While I am sure there are people who have used prostitution for other reasons, I never saw it at the prison. Women who were addicted to drugs but who hadn't been abused might rob, steal, lie or cheat, but having sex for money wasn't one of the things they would do. It isn't because it was beneath them. It is that usually our choice of crime is reflective of what is also going on with us now and has gone on with us in the past. It isn't that the crime reflects what was done to them as much as it will be reflective of what or how they felt as a child.

People who are schizoid may often attempt to narrow the complexity of the world by engaging in sex with as many people who they regularly come into contact with as they can. It is a way of narrowing the complexity of relationships. Some folks who are not schizoid will do a similar thing for reasons that may be much more complex, but in the end their actions produce the same result. If a person believes that others are as interested in sex as they are, then having contact with folks who they have sex with makes the world less scary.

Everyone has met people who are promiscuous or adulterous. Once these people have dealt with their sexual shame, they can then choose their sexual behaviors rather than doing so in such an automated way. Until they deal with their sexual shame, the likelihood is very great that they would continue their promiscuity and/or their extramarital sex. They would also be very vulnerable to others who were expressing or feeling sexual shame themselves since such persons tend to attract one another.

There are of course folks who would qualify for being antisocial in their sexual behavior so that they simply show little restraint. Their behavior isn't as motivated by shame as it is by self-interest. Folks like that are going to express their antisocial ways in other areas of their life, not just in one area.

Adult sexuality expressed even between partners can be done for various reasons during various times. As human beings we are capable of having lots of reasons for our behavior and sometimes multiple reasons with the same person and even in the same event.

Protecting yourself is first being aware of the emotion and perhaps the deeper reason for it being expressed in your presence. Recognizing the multiple reasons for someone expressing sexual feelings in your presence gives you more options and allows you to recognize that it may not have anything to do with you personally.

However, if you are responding to the sexual feelings then that is also a great message to you about your level of sexual shame or vulnerability to it. Either way it is better to know so that you can take steps to stay safe.

Most of the time, when you become aware that the sexual feelings that are expressed in your presence have little to do with you, it is easy to stay safe. It is only when a person has believed that the emotions were directed toward them that it is more difficult to choose more wisely.

A second way of staying safe is knowing whether you are feeling your feelings or someone else's. If the person who you are having these feelings with is not someone who you would normally have been attracted to, it is likely the feelings started as not yours. What I normally ask the person is whether they were feeling sexual before the person entered the room. Or I might ask if the person they are having these feelings around is like any of their past sexual partners or anyone they have wanted as a sexual partner. Any yes answer makes determining whether it is you or them a little more difficult. So I advise students to know who the people are and the types of people who they normally find attractive in the first place. That way they can be more careful on the front end of those folks. It usually is only a small number of people who anyone would have such strong feelings about on their own. It usually would also have to do with the person reminding them of a person or persons in their past.

If the person you are with who is sloshing sexual feelings is outwardly doing something that can be addressed, then doing so will probably change the emotional content coming your direction. For instance, if someone is sloshing sexual feelings and they are quick to touch you even in a so called safe way, your commenting about their touching you might be all that would be required to stop the feelings coming your direction.

The same is true of inappropriate comments. Things that are said with double meanings that have a sexual implication can easily be commented upon which can change the course of the encounter.

The reason I haven't spoken first about how to deal with this through the use of emotions is that I believe this method is more dangerous and would require you first to have the safety of knowing and using the above examples to deal with the toxic emotions. It is in part that knowing what prompts the sexuality puts it in the frame where you can more easily deal with it safely.

In order to use your emotions to deal with others, you could choose an emotion, like confidence. Then to use the emotion, you would start by thinking about it so that you can really feel it, then keep that confidence in your mind but don't try to show the other person that you are feeling confident. Just hold the feeling for yourself. This would block the feelings the other person is sending to you. Interestingly, not only might it block what is coming at you, it also might be encouraging to the other person. The danger or difficulty is that sometimes confidence isn't a wall of safety but an invitation to some people because confidence is so attractive. However, if you held forgiveness in your mind and didn't show it, then you could help them to feel forgiveness as well as protect yourself from their emotions, of guilt and shame. That is what healing is about.

CHAPTER 10

PROTECTING YOURSELF FROM OTHER PEOPLE'S SEXUAL FEELINGS

*"If there is one 'constant' in the structure and
theme of the wonder tale, it is transformation. "*

Jack Zipes, The Oxford Companion to Fairy Tales

Gerald: I don't understand what has come over me. For the first time in my life I have sexual feelings that are out of the blue. I love my wife and don't want to hurt her. What is going on with me?

Therapist: Let me ask you some questions, before I answer any questions. OK? I don't want to answer before I am certain of what is going on. Tell me, is the person who you are having these feelings for someone who is your type?

Gerald: That is just it. Normally, I wouldn't be interested in someone like her at all. She is attractive all right but normally, people like her have only been people who I was friends with. You know it makes me wonder about myself. I don't know what is going

63

on with me. Why would I suddenly start having sexual feelings for a woman who works for me?

Therapist: Gerald I am going to also not answer your question until I can understand it better. Have you and your wife had any difficulty with sex, or in getting along? Or are there any other major changes going on right now in your life?

Gerald: My wife and I get along well. If anything sex is better than it has ever been before business is great and we as a couple have fewer things to worry about, the kids are all doing well and grown. That is just it Doc. It feels crazy like something that is out of my control.

Therapist: You say you have been feeling out of control, when did it start?

Gerald: Well that is just it. I first noticed it in Carol's presence. I began to see what she said, and how she talked as incredibly sexy. I started avoiding her and that didn't help any either. I even started having dreams about having sex with her. I have never done that since being an adolescent. Am I cracking up ?

Therapist: Gerald I am pretty sure that you are fine, but let me ask some more questions so that I can really know how fine that you are. Ok. I do need to ask you whether you have sexual shame that you never forgave yourself for.

Gerald: No….

Therapist: Really?

Gerald: Well when I was young I used to look at pornographic pictures and videos. I haven't for a long time but I do still feel guilty for that.

Therapist: Ok, now when you have been in Carol's presence and you felt those sexual feelings, how much were they similar to the feelings of shame?

Gerald: Hmm. That is odd. I...well you have something there. I feel sexual feelings like I did when I was a teenager looking at the porn. That is part of what is so upsetting about all of this.

Therapist: And Carol is the first person you remember having any type of sexual feelings with like this?

Gerald: Yes. It seemed to come out of the blue and has been so powerful that I felt almost like I was in the ocean with the waves hitting me.

Therapist: As if you were no longer in control?

Gerald: Yes. That is it exactly.

Therapist: I can't be absolutely positive but it sounds like Carol has sexual shame and is sloshing those feelings in your presence. She may be doing that because she may simply feel very safe in your presence and be letting go of those feelings of sexual shame. Then you experience those feelings as just sexual feelings. And this all happens because she feels safe in your presence.

Gerald: You mean like a little girl feeling safe to have a crush on her teacher because she knows that the teacher is safe?

Therapist: That is almost perfect. In fact, it may more so than you think. Her sexual shame may be from when she was a little girl, and she may be having shame in your presence because she feels safe around you. Back when I worked in the women's prison I could easily guess at what age a woman had been sexually abused because under pressure she would revert to that emotional age in some form or fashion so that she actually had mannerisms of a child of that age. I was almost always right.

Gerald: That is difficult to believe.

Therapist: Yes, I know. However, when a woman or man heals I can't tell anything. It is as if their unconscious is pleading with the world to help them heal. When they do heal there is no sign of abuse or reverting to the age when the abuse began.

Gerald: So it is some form of the sexual shame being manifested in their body?

Therapist: That is absolutely right. In fact, we even had women who had gone through traumatic events whose bodies would literally demonstrate the trauma. We had one woman who had been strangled until being unconscious by a man who she was terrified would kill her. If she talked about the incident, red marks would appear on her throat that looked like hands strangling her. It wasn't just my imagination, others saw and were amazed by the woman's markings when she talked about it. I testified about this and other things about her to a judge who was considering letting her go. It would have been the right thing to do, but the judge wouldn't do it even though he wrote to the parole board urging them to. We had other women who also had marks that would appear when they talked about their abuse. One had a hand print that would appear on her face very prominently if she discussed the trauma of being beaten by her ex-husband.

Gerald: That is bazaar.

Therapist: Or you could think of it as that we as human beings are not just a body with a mind, but a mind body that is so interconnected that it is sometimes difficult to tell one from the other. Actually, neuroscience backs up these forms of expression through the body.

Commentary

We have dealt with at least one way of dealing with the sexual feelings that are picked up that don't belong to us. When we interpret them in the above way they are more easily dealt with and the meaning is changed from being a sexual emotion to one of shame that comes out as sexual. The number of times I have seen someone who was having sexual feelings that were not their own is way over the top. Several keys are that this is a person who we would not normally find sexually attractive, even if attractive. But more of the keys are in the questions asked of Gerald.

I would like to deal now with what to do when the person's behavior is inappropriate but not so inappropriate as to be something that could be easily addressed. For instance, dressing in revealing ways, sitting in a dress so that you have a clear view up their dress, or a male sitting in such a way that promptly displays his genital area in a way that is difficult to ignore.

When someone is dressed in ways that we think are inappropriate but still socially acceptable, we have a dilemma. We don't know if it is our prudishness or their inappropriateness. Any response we find inside of ourselves can tell us about us even if it may not tell us much about the other person.

Let's admit that a very attractive man or woman who is dressing in ways that are very appealing to us is something that we can appreciate. However, we usually know when there is something more going on than just being in the presence of someone who is attractive. Usually if it is just an attractive person being themselves, there won't be any sexual feelings present unless those feelings are ours because they are the type of person we tend to find attractive. Otherwise, it is much more likely that the feeling you would be having would be intimidation, jealousy, unattractiveness, old, or ignored if it is just about their attractiveness.

When someone sits, stands, or drapes their body in suggestive ways or is more revealing of their body by how they are sitting, something else may be going on that has far more to do with their sexual shame than with any sexual feelings being intentionally passed.

Earlier in my work, I believed that speaking directly to the inappropriateness of the way the person was sitting, standing or the like would change things. So I would tell them when there were others present so that I would be safe and it would be clear what I was communicating. It never worked well and actually tended to make it worse. While I was never accused of it being my dirty mind since I always had someone else present, it still didn't change the behavior. It only caused the person to become anxious and try to not change it consciously, which would only work for as long as they were thinking about it.

You see, a situation like this is a double bind. If you address it in a direct way, as stated above, it is wrong; and if you don't address it, it is wrong because you continue to feel awkward. What worked better was addressing the double bind when it was occurring. This third option is healing to the person and takes care of you at the same time. For instance, the following occurred countless times at the prison. I would be in a group setting with 7 or 8 women and the one directly across the room from me would be sitting with her legs apart as if she had pants on, yet she was wearing a dress. I would simply ask another woman in the group to change chairs with me, without giving any explanation for how come. I would have chosen someone who was at a side angle to the woman who was sitting inappropriately. When asked how come I had done that I would then say. "So that I can be a gentleman to ________". She often didn't do it again. However, she would continue to do other things that were equally inappropriate until she healed of the sexual shame she had for the abuse that was done to her. When she was healed it was automatic that she simply wouldn't do it anymore. It was a simple as that.

My saying "So that I could be a gentleman" allowed me to be one. It got the issue in the room, kept me safe, and more importantly allowed the woman and anyone else present to see another way of addressing dilemmas that are double binds.

Another behavior that is often difficult to know how to address would be a person of same or opposite sex touching your body on places that are not thought of as sexual (i.e. hand, arm, cheek, back, shoulders, etc.) but the touch has a sexual air to it. This might be because either sexual feelings are communicated through the touch or because the touch is held too long, or sensuously, etc. I have had both men and women do this and I am not sure which is more difficult to deal with because both same and opposite sex can generate specific difficulties. While the gender that usually attracts us may pose one sort of dilemma so too does the other gender that we normally don't find ourselves attracted to. I am not talking just about the shock that we might feel when encountering sexual feelings from or toward a person who we normally wouldn't find any attraction. It is also some of the added complexity of discerning what might be the ulterior meaning of the action. When it is someone of the gender we normally are attracted to, we may be more alert to seduction, manipulation, etc. However, for the same reasons we may not be as aware of the ulterior motives of the person who is opposite the gender we normally find ourselves attracted to. Either way, you might be surprised what more you discover about yourself just by exploring it emotionally in your mind.

Over the years, I have learned about the subtleties of how males touch each other to control, to direct, and to give them an edge of leadership that has nothing to do with sex, but everything to do with power.

One man who used his height and his outgoing personality to mask that he used touch to give him more power with other males. He would put his arm around you as if he was your friend when he asked you for something that he knew was a stretch. The way he worked was that he would be genial and then when the two of you and others were getting up to go into another room, he would slide up to you. Then he would put his arm around you and ask you to do a favor for him that you could do in your official capacity. The touch was supposed to be familiar, like what friends would do, so that you would say yes. He only did that once with me as the look I gave him for putting his arm around me said, that I didn't appreciate it. If he had ignored it then I would have openly said,"Please don't touch me. I don't like to be touched". I have said that a number of times. It puts the entire displeasure on me, and isn't blaming, pointing the finger, or in any way overtly accusing the other person. It does, however, address the behavior. That is the secret to effective dealing with this type of inappropriate behavior, to openly address it but with indirectness by accepting the uncomfortable feelings as your own. In this way, it is similar to the earlier method of wanting to be a gentleman.

The way women seem to use touch to evoke power is more subtle, and seems to utilize different implied meanings. With men it is implied that you would want to remain one of the guys or that to disagree would invite rejection. With women it seems more to be not about threats but about implied closeness and trustworthiness.

It really doesn't matter whether the intent is to gain power, express anger and control, get attention, or avoid criticism. We can deal with each of these behavior in similar ways. When someone passes sexual feelings along with a touch, it can be unsettling; but again, it is either because of their shame and their desire for power, attention, and revenge or it is their way of avoiding criticism. If it was really only about sexual feelings then it wouldn't be happening unless you had already made it clear that a sexual advance was ok.

In prison one way of gaining the upper hand is by stumbling or accidentally tripping so that you have to touch the other person to avoid falling. Because touch makes a person feel more known, accepted and safe, it also makes them easier to manipulate in the future. So finding ways of touching others is a powerful way for folks to make someone more vulnerable to being exploited. When they also have sexual feelings on their mind and then express remorse for their covert act it also masks what they are doing and it tells them something about their victim. An honest person won't welcome the touch a second time that has sexuality infused into it. That person may be still vulnerable but not as much as with the double bind of the implied sexual feelings that make the touch more confusing. The person who appears to be happy to see them a second time is already telling them that they responded to the sexual feelings and liked it. They are an easy touch. Ok, bad pun, but hopefully a good reminder.

CHAPTER 11

ALCHEMY FOR OTHER PEOPLE'S GUILT

*"I don't know these stories as well as
they know me, I've discovered. "*

Joan Gould

*"His own image; no longer a dark, gray bird, ugly and
disagreeable to look at, but a graceful and beautiful
swan. To be born in a duck's nest, in a farmyard, is of no
consequence to a bird, if it is hatched from a swan's egg. "*

Hans Christian Andersen, <u>The Ugly Duckling</u>

Going through the streets of some cities in Europe where begging seems to be almost everywhere, I noticed differences between when I felt compelled to give and when I just felt irritated and insulted.

The insulted feeling was the easiest to recognize. It usually meant that someone was acting in such a way as to evoke feelings of guilt and a desire to help. Only a much trained actor can pur-posely project feelings that would be picked up by and even felt by others the way the actor wanted you to feel. The person who is truly feeling needy is typically embarrassed about it. Usually with these beggars, I would notice that on the surface they would ap-pear needy, but the feelings I got from them were more of dis-gust, contempt, and anger. They also appeared to be very kind and passive, but this also seemed to be just on the surface. The emotions they were sending were very unpleasant. Some folks who don't know how they tend to respond to begging could easily be confused by the unpleasant feelings and conclude that they were having negative feelings about the person who was begging. They would tend to feel guilty about those feelings, and thus give more freely. The beggars who were holding that type of disgust so that as you walked by you would likely feel disgust were effective with certain people. Frequently, these beggars would position them-selves in front of a church. When you first came out of the church you would see them and presumably be moved to give. Since many Christians have such guilt already it wasn't much of a stretch to exploit that feeling.

There were also beggars who had dogs with them, and they seemed to be equally divided between those having happy thoughts and emotions appreciative of whatever people gave and those who were using the dogs to get sympathy and more money. The folks who seemed happy and loving toward their dogs did seem to re-ceive lots of money. The ones who appeared to be just exploiting the dogs got less money. They, like the beggars at the churches, tried too hard and were acting in ways to evoke emotions in you so that you would give. They didn't do so well, and again their anger was just below the surface.

However, one of the most powerful ways to manipulate others is by broadcasting a sense of guilt and responsibility at the same time while taking no responsibility yourself. It is what gets parents, children, partners, unsuspecting tourists, and passersby. When you examine what the feelings are that you tend to feel when passing by someone who is begging, what are they? Do you feel sorry for them? Do you feel a little guilty because you have something and they don't? Do you feel more than a little bit responsible for them? If you answered yes to these, then Hallelujah you are a decent person.

Decent folks tend to respond with their own guilt, responsibility, or sadness about not being able to help.

Truly needy people tend to give off a sense of guilt for being as bad off as they are, and they also tend to give off a sense of responsibility that they don't want to take for their situation. Of course they feel guilt, who wouldn't? Also, who would want to continue to feel guilt? A person would search for ways to stop feeling so much guilt all the time for their situation. When people feel victimized they often don't want to be responsible so they give those feelings off. It isn't a conscious act but they seem to do so. When this victimization becomes routine, then it begins to happen totally without their knowledge. It can have a powerful effect on us. It can grab our attention, and evoke our care, or guilt enough to be compelling.

My hunch is that folks that are doing this have no idea of the fact that they are sending off emotions, they are simply expressing the dilemma they feel. They don't see a way to get or be what they want, or they are so demoralized that they don't' believe it is possible anymore. The double bind they feel is so palpable that if you are very sensitive you will pick it up as well. Some of them exploit it all the time. We had women at the prison who you could count on to exploit, use, manipulate and solicit from any volunteers who came into the institution. They were really good at being pitiful, and giving off both guilt and responsibility. Volunteers had to be repeatedly instructed to not bring in things to the inmates. Since I knew they would be that way with volunteers that came into the prison I used that in order to teach volunteers how to behave and how to stay safe. The volunteers were so vulnerable to hearing how sad the women's situations were and to feeling the guilt and responsibility to fix it that they were very easy targets. For some volunteers, the rules didn't apply to them. For others, the powerful feelings of need, desire, or hurt, fear, or dysfunction caused them to want to give, do, or help in some way that went beyond the rules. I had lots of arguments with well-meaning volunteers who wanted to do things that the institution banned or give things that were banned. They saw and felt a need by the inmates and wanted to do something for them. They felt the inmate's feelings and wanted to help.

When they broke the rules, the volunteers would justify their actions by saying, but it was only a _______ it doesn't cost very much at all. Why can't I give it to them? Or better yet, I have been doing this for a while and nothing bad has happened, so why is it wrong? I would have to explain to the volunteers that their tendency to want to help in those ways not only wasn't helping, it was also making the inmates more dependent not less. Usually, the volunteers would learn to respond in a better way and often then so too did the inmates.

While the technique I am about to offer won't help with exploitive folks who are just scamming you, it will help with family, friends, and close acquaintances that give over those same feelings of guilt and responsibility so that everyone seems to want to help them. Part of the dilemma is that by helping we are continuing the problem. While it may be helpful to us to help strangers, especially if they somehow pulled our heart strings; when our family and close friends do it, we really can do something better to deal with them than help by doing things for them.

The reason that we tend to feel so responsible and so much guilt is because that is what is being offered to us. When honest folks are giving us their responsibility and their guilt, they can walk away and feel better because they "of course can't do it on their own. " Because they don't believe in themselves we can give back the responsibility and guilt while we then follow it up with confidence.

The way it would work is that while talking with the person who doesn't believe in themselves and you feel responsible to help and a little bit guilty that you don't want to or that you didn't before, you can emotionally give those feelings back and then begin to feel confidence and not show it. In this way, they begin to first feel their own feelings of responsibility and then they get a dose of belief in themselves through you. However, because you are simply feeling the confidence you have in them, they will feel it too and probably not know that you helped them to have it in the first place.

The result is that they begin to feel more responsible for themselves and believe that they can do something about their situation. They can of course, especially when they realize that they have both the responsibility as well as the confidence that they can do something. Your believing in them will make a difference.

Recently I read about how neuroscience recognizes that your positive feelings can powerfully impact a person sitting across from you. Not only can you give back the feelings that will motivate them, you can give them the sense of confidence that will make the big difference where they can go back and do something better.

If you are in a negative trance and I go into a positive one in your presence, it is as if I am lending you my antenna to draw in better reception of recognizing your natural strengths, abilities, and options. It isn't going to happen right away but it happens eventually.

The deeper that I go into a positive trance in your presence, the deeper that you can go and draw on your own resources. One of the things that is absolutely true is that you already have the solutions to your problems inside of you, whether you know the path yet or not. Your strengths and abilities you rediscover along the way will suffice for you to make a major difference in your life. When you treat others and especially your family that way, you will notice that they will rise to the occasion.

CHAPTER 12

YOUR FEELINGS CAN BE A WINDOW INTO ANOTHER PERSON'S SOUL

*"Don't be afraid to grow up, Peter. It's
only a trap if you forget how to fly. "*

Jorge Enrique Ponce, <u>Grounded : The Untold
story of Peter pan and Captain Hook</u>

Using your feelings as a sign, clue, or marker to let you know what is going on with your partner, colleague, child, student, teacher, friend, or associate gives you lots of other options for keeping you safe and being able to either deepen the relationship or allow it to become more effective and viable.

While this book has been suggesting this concept throughout, this chapter will be directly and specifically addressing how it is that the emotions we feel give us clues about what is going on with others. Some of the time when we have been feeling tired, angry, fearful, or joyful it is because someone else near us has been feeling one of those feelings powerfully. However, the direct exchange of emotions that is a window into others' feelings doesn't work in all cases, even if it is a good rule of thumb to begin with.

Yes of course, as previously suggested there are times you experience emotions of sexuality because the person you have been talking with has sexual shame that is coming out in that fashion, even if they would not by any stretch of the imagination say they were feeling sexual. Your awareness of someone else's sexual feelings certainly doesn't mean that is what they were feeling.

Some of the time when you have been feeling irritation with others, it may mean that someone is really wanting your attention whether you are interested in providing that or not. Often when a child is needy for attention, the target feeling that parents, siblings and others receive from the child would be irritation. It is one of those clear cut markers that I take as a message.

When at the prison I found myself being irritated with someone it was almost always the case that one or more of the people near me were feeling needy and wanting more attention. It isn't just my response but the response of many people to a neediness for attention. Perhaps we don't (as a society) tolerate people having emotional needs very well, but it is almost universal that when a person begins to feel irritation the first thing I would be looking at would be their sense of need for attention. Of course the person needing attention may do distracting things which we could label as irritating. If all we did was do that it would simply lead to more frustration on both our part as well as the needy person's part.

When we address the need for attention by giving it, not only will our irritation diminish, but also the person who was feeling needy would begin to act more compliant. Their lack of compliance, or irritating behaviors such as making noise, going extra slow, etc. would dramatically change. It usually won't change until they are more satisfied with the level of attention they received. If you detected that someone near you was feeling that needy by recognizing your own feelings, you would have helped both yourself and the person you directly helped as well as anyone nearby.

When you out of the blue began to feel as if the people around you were challenging you and your authority, you could redouble your efforts and become more direct and firm about what you wanted, as well as what you expected. If you did that it might even work for a short time but ultimately it wouldn't. The reason is that the person giving off the feelings you experienced as irritation was needing to feel more powerful. If the only thing that you did was to fuss at them or to criticize them, they might comply for a little while, but ultimately they wouldn't comply and their ability to frustrate you with their negative responses or their passive aggressive responses would be over the top.

Finding ways to assist that person to have more of a sense of personal power will help greatly. It would have to be in a form of an experience and not simply told to them. Additionally, by being somewhat rebellious and demanding more power and authority they are posing a double bind to you. Giving in to them is a problem and so too is simply saying no. It is much more complicated than that.

You can respond to the double binds that their rebellious behavior along with their demand for more autonomy create, unbeknownst to them. They have no clue that they are offering a double bind. They probably don't even know that a double bind offers only two options, of which neither one would be good. The only way out of the double bind is to avoid the double bind and address other things so that they get to be ok, and you have avoided either giving in or saying no.

When you are around people who seem to have hurt you or are hurting you by their behavior, it is easy enough to figure that they either have been hurt by you or someone who you look like or are a stand-in for. Either way, their anger, hurt, and desire for revenge isn't going to stop just because you want it to. While it is true that if you are feeling hurt they were likely feeling hurt as well, that doesn't mean that you did anything to hurt them. You, however, have the opportunity to help them by offering new and different ways of coping with those feelings.

Unfortunately, the hurt that someone wants to get revenge to cope with isn't going to go away through any revenge. Revenge might be satisfying initially, but that satisfaction doesn't last. Holding a grudge comes out toward others whether we want it to or not.

However, if you are in the presence of someone and you feel ready to just give up, then that feeling is a great indicator that the person you are with has already given up. They don't see their abilities very clearly and have probably already given up so they actually seem to give off that air. People in their presence tend to give up, and agree that they can't.

Let's get to some more practical applications of this. For instance, when your partner is feeling hurt but not showing it on his or her face, and you know that you are certainly hurt. It is a good indication that they have been feeling every bit as hurt as you are. In fact, one good rule of thumb would be that if you have been feeling pain at a level of 7 following a fight, is it very likely the person you fought with is feeling the same level 7 of pain.

If you have been feeling a little bit alienated or you sense a distance between you and your partner, while you might ask if that is going on, there are other options as well. For instance, if you have been wanting more closeness emotionally and when talking with them, then you could assume that they are too, even if they don't seem to act upon that in the way you would like for them to. Lots of times couples will both want more closeness but it is defined in different ways and with different behaviors that prove it. Characteristically, men would prefer to be shown that they are loved by their partner wanting them sexually. It isn't about sex as much as it is about validating them as a person who their partner desires. Being wanted and believed in is something that all of us want. Women often ask for and want to be affirmed in different ways, but they still want the affirmation. They still want the acknowledgement of them as a person. They still want to feel close. So if you are wanting to feel closer to your partner it is a good bet that they want that too. They just may or may not want it demonstrated in the same ways.

CHAPTER 13

CHANGING HOW YOU FEEL

""But he has nothing on at all," said a little child at last. "Good heavens! Listen the voice of an innocent child," said the farmer, and one whispered to the other what the child had said. "But he has nothing on at all," cried at last the whole people. That made a deep impression upon the emperor, for it seemed to him that they were right; but he thought to himself, "Now I must bear up to the end." And the chamberlains walked with still greater dignity, as if they carried the train which did not exist. "

Hans Christian Andersen, <u>The Emperor's New Clothes</u>

"His own image; no longer a dark, gray bird, ugly and disagreeable to look at, but a graceful and beautiful swan. To be born in a duck's nest, in a farmyard, is of no consequence to a bird, if it is hatched from a swan's egg. "

Hans Christian Andersen, <u>The Ugly Duckling</u>

Changing how you feel is the focus of Psychotherapy. It may have been invented to help us all take more control of how we feel. It has probably been being practiced for as long as people have been around. As such, there are some tools that most of us know and use all the time. When a tool works, there is no reason to look for anything else. However, when it doesn't work and we keep feeling a way that we don't want to feel, there are some tricks that can change our experience. While there are a lot of tricks that others offer that work, as best as I can I will only mention the ones that I came up with on my own. I would rather offer approaches that I have developed or learned on my own, so that I am not duplicating anything that anyone else offers. Part of the reason to not duplicate things offered is that if I was to address all the possible ways to change how we feel that Psychology has offered, then the book would be very long indeed. Instead, by offering only the ideas that are direct outgrowth of my approach, then the book can be consistent as well as much more manageable.

Susie: You act as if I can simply change how I feel. If I could do that I certainly would. Have you ever had an anxiety attack? No one would keep feeling that way if they knew how to easily stop.

Dr. Lentz: You are right. It is unreasonable that anyone under normal conditions would choose to have an anxiety attack. However, it is very possible to help people to stop having anxiety attacks with techniques. You have been changing your feelings since you were a child. You have far more ability to do so than you may recognize.

Susie: Like what? What could possibly help with an anxiety attack?

Dr. Lentz: Knowing things about anxiety that would help you to feel and think differently about it. For instance it is probably your friend rather than an enemy. The very approach of only trying to get away from the feeling probably made it more difficult to do so. Actually, it is a process that involves understanding what a person does that isn't likely to get the anxiety to leave, as well as what can be done. For instance, when you realize that anxiety may be a signal from your unconscious letting you know that there is danger that you are not addressing, then this would change everything, would it not?

Susie: Well yes. But it is hard to believe that something that is so terrible is actually attempting to do something good. What good could possibly come from anxiety?

Dr. Lentz: Well I have known people who discovered that their anxiety often meant that someone was attempting to manipulate them. Others discovered that their anxiety was recognizing an emotional danger because somehow they intuited that the business they worked at was shutting down, and no one knew about it at the business but somehow they knew. One man was feeling anxious and having anxiety attacks because he was not able to do his job and he could tell that people were unhappy with him. Ultimately, when the business split his duties so that two people would do them instead of just him, he calmed down because he realized that he wasn't going to be fired.

Susie: You are saying that all those people were having anxiety and that somehow they stopped having anxiety when they discovered what they were not seeing?

Dr. Lentz: Yes, and no. Each of the people I just mentioned had anxiety attacks, not just anxiety. It was something that was very powerful for each of them when they discovered that their anxiety was actually trying to get them to see something and take steps to be safe.

Susie: So how come I have anxiety?

Dr. Lentz: That is easy. You tend to see things that are a problem in the world and then you look inside yourself for the problem. Because we can almost always find things to blame ourselves for, you have found lots of things that you took responsibility for. If you begin to allow any sense of anxiety to be a clue for you to look at things and people outside of yourself for the problem and then seek to find solutions for the problems you discover, then your anxiety would disappear.

Susie: Ok, well what about not feeling repelled by my boyfriend? Do you have an easy fix for that? I broke up with him because I was repelled by being near him. I still feel terrible because it must be something about me that made me push him away. He was such a decent person and here I seemed to go to great lengths to get rid of him. Would there have been an easy fix?

Dr. Lentz: No, unfortunately, your anxiety may well have been telling you that he wasn't as good as he seemed on the surface. From what you have told me previously, I suspect he was someone who had a porn addiction and your anxiety and uncomfortableness was your unconscious's way of alerting you and keeping you safe. While I can't be 100% sure, I am way over 90% certain that he was a sex addict. Women who are dating sex addicts who are using a lot of porn often begin to think there is something wrong with themselves just like you did, and then they become almost obsessed with finding something wrong with themselves exactly like you did.

Susie: Let's assume that you are right for now, how will I know?

Dr. Lentz: That one is both easy and impossible. It is easy because the more that you begin to check your intuition every time you are feeling some sort of anxiety the more you will likely discover that you are pretty accurate with some exceptions. However, for you to know for sure with your ex-boyfriend would be more difficult. Unless he tells you it may be pretty difficult to know. However, if you push all men away then that would be an indication it was you and not the boyfriend. You don't push all men away, just ones that are porn addicts who are too nice or too sweet to be believed.

Susie: Ok, you are convincing me about some of this, but I will want to think about it a lot more. In the past I have had trouble with feeling depressed. I suppose you are going to tell me that it is easy to overcome feelings of depression. The TV is full of ads for some sort of antidepressant. Surely you are not going to tell me that my feelings of depression were also something good?

Dr. Lentz: Sorry to disappoint you, but having feelings of depression is often useful for more than just selling anti-depression medication. Often depression is a sign that we are feeling very fearful or at least have been. When a person has been feeling very fearful for a while, the cortisol that is emptied into the bloodstream is not good for the entire body. Guess what is a natural way of corralling the cortisol?

Susie: Surely you are not going to say depression?

Dr. Lentz: Actually, I am. Depression is the body's way of protecting you from some of the harmful effects of cortisol over time. It is a smoking gun for knowing that someone has been through a difficult period and/or may still be in it. In part because one portion of the depression is a response to impossible situations that we experience as double binds. When a person is in a double bind, they see only two options. One option is bad and the other is worse. When a person is caught up in that sort of thinking, they can't see any other options and so they tend to make bad decisions. It is one of the reasons that folks commit suicide. They simply don't see any other options. When they are able to see their options, they are able to raise their mood and feel fine.

Susie: This is all sounding too pat. It is as if information fixes any emotions that a person has. Just knowing things hasn't always helped. It didn't help when my father died or when my mother was so awful to me.

Dr. Lentz: You are right. Information is only one of the ways that we can raise our mood or change how we feel. It may be the easiest, but it is only one way. We can also change how we feel by adding other emotions. One example would be when a person is feeling fear. It is possible to alter the fear by adding in humor, joy, sadness, or even shock. When the feeling of fear is also connected to humor it is going to change things. The same is true about shock, joy, or sadness. It is like having a vanilla milkshake and adding in strawberries, chocolate, or blueberries. The addition would change the milkshake powerfully.

Susie: Ok, on the surface that makes sense. You seem to be saying that emotions can be transformed into something other than what we have been feeling instead of attempting to get away from them.

Dr. Lentz: That is the principle in a nutshell. Respecting the fact that your body and history produced the emotion you were feeling is a way of also respecting yourself. Of course, emotions are not always giving us factual data. They are giving us sensations that either pushes us away or draws us near. It isn't like emotions are something that can be trusted in the sense of being truthful. They are simply emotions, and as such, they are offering us clues about our environment.

Susie: Ok, so how do we change those feelings that are so unpleasant that it is difficult to experience them?

Dr. Lentz: Like what feelings?

Susie: Like jealousy, envy, anger, disgust, and dislike. What about those feelings. How are we going to change them?

Dr. Lentz: First, instead of trying only to get away from them I am going to encourage you to be more respectful of yourself. Jealousy and envy can only be occurring if a person is not recognizing and respecting what is going on right with themselves and they are comparing themselves to someone else at the same time. Almost any comparison between one person and another person ends in the one doing the comparing being very unhappy. If today they declare themselves better than the other person, it is only so long before they will feel bad because they will discover someone who is better than them soon enough. It really happens outside of our awareness that if we are judging others then we are judging ourselves on the same criteria, and this judging won't feel good. One man I know who is very bright and extremely capable sets himself up by expecting that he can still do what he did mentally 30 years earlier. He also thinks he should be able to do what he did physically 30 years ago, even if it takes him longer. He has un-realistic expectations of himself. I expect some of it is because he finds faults in others as they don't live up to what he thinks that they should be doing. It has cost him a tremendous amount of joy and happiness.

Susie: Ok, I get that. Are you saying that I could have changed my feelings about my boyfriend? It sounds as if you are saying that if I just worked at it I could have changed how I feel.

Dr. Lentz: Technically, you could, but practically it may not have been either wise or helpful. If you could have changed how you feel about him, how would that have helped? His behavior was going to be a problem. Feelings give us information and we do well to pay attention even if they are contaminated feelings. For example one man I worked with was unhappy with his girl-friend and was having feelings for another woman. Thankfully, he was willing to investigate what was going on before he simply broke up with her. The woman he was interested in was virtually a clone of his girlfriend. Breaking up with the one and going with the other would only have been like the dog chasing it's tail as Proverbs says, and that happens when we only follow our feelings.

Susie: So what are you saying? Are you saying that doing what I felt like doing was wrong?

Dr. Lentz: No. What you did was wise. You felt feelings and also got information about what they were telling you. That is being very smart. It is like double checking your intuition. Just because you think someone is trustworthy doesn't mean that they are, and when it feels like someone is wrong or hurtful, double checking how you are experiencing them is a very wise thing to do.

Susie: So you are not blaming me for leaving my boyfriend?

Dr. Lentz: No. In fact, your feelings were helping to keep you safe in that instance, but the only way you can keep your intuition sharp is to keep checking it out. However, I am saying that if your feelings are getting in the way, then it is easy enough to change them. For instance, if you wanted to eat broccoli because of the nutrients in it but you didn't like it because of childhood experiences, then it would not be that big of a deal to change to eating and enjoying broccoli. The same would be true if you had fallen out of love with your husband and wanted to fall back in love with him. If he wasn't a jerk and the ways the two of you had interacted had caused you to drift apart, then it would be no big deal to remedy the problem. It would be harder if one of you had fallen in love with another person during the drift, but that too could be overcome if everyone was interested in doing that.

Susie: Are you saying that a person could even change their interest in sex?

Dr. Lentz: Yes. It is very possible to change lots of things about sexual interest; however, once someone has an interest it isn't easily blocked or extinguished. For instance once someone has developed a fetish for ostrich feathers, then it would be very difficult to extinguish that interest. The person could discover other ways to be happy but they would likely retain some interest in ostrich feathers. I think this idea was some of how come people believed they could change sexual preferences of homosexuals who wanted to change and be heterosexual. The clinicians were not recognizing that extinguishing the interest that was there already would be very difficult. The whole argument between whether someone has chosen to be homosexual or if they were born homosexual was missing the point. Sexual preference is much more complicated than choosing, and yet, it is also not simply an inborn fact either.

In spite of the fact that people feel as if they were born with an interest on way or the other, it is much more complicated than that. There is no scientific evidence that people are born homosexual or heterosexual; however, that doesn't mean that they aren't either. It just means that feelings are not something that can be that empirically trusted. Just because people believed that people would never be able to fly didn't mean that it was true.

Susie: That is all well, and you've answered more than I was asking. Are you saying that people can change their interest in sex?

Dr. Lentz: So you are asking me if it is possible to become interested or more interested in sex when you haven't been for a while?

Susie: Yes, I want to know if people can change their interest or their level of desire for sex.

Dr. Lentz : The short answer is yes; however, it also depends upon a number of the beliefs the person has and the reason that they lost interest. It is something that we could look at for you or someone else personally, but the basic answer is yes.

The other answer is that changing how we feel is mostly a matter of noticing how we feel and what we do to feel that way. Then we can change what we are doing to maintain those feelings so another feeling can be experienced. For instance, when a person is afraid of flying, they have to focus upon negative images, experiences, or negative possibilities to maintain that fear. They also have to notice the feelings that happen when they dwell upon images of planes falling from the sky. The feelings that follow this negative focus are predictable, as are the feelings when changing what is being dwelled upon. If you dwell on images of a baby deer, puppy, horse, or even a baby cat, there will be different feelings because the images of those animals brings a smile to most people's face.

Susie: So you are saying that I can change my level of interest in sex?

Dr. Lentz: Yes, however, it also has to do with the relationship. Feelings can change, and yet inside of a relationship there can be mistakes and miscommunications, just like you and I have had before. However, it is way more complicated to look at how to change sexual feelings so that you are more interested. It involves your relationship, past, likes, and dislikes, as well as your growing sense of who you see yourself becoming.

In the end, Susie did change her sexual feelings. She, however, also changed her partner.

Amen, D. G. (2000). *Change your brain,* change *your life: The break-through program for conquering anxiety, depression, obsessiveness, anger, and impulsiveness.* New York, NY: Times Books.

Bannink, F. (2014). *Post traumatic success: Positive psychology and solution-focused strategies to help clients survive and thrive.* New York, NY: W. W. Norton & Company.

Borysenko, Joan, Minding the Body, Mending the Mind, (1988) New York, NY: Bantam Books.

Carlson, Jon, Englar-Carlson Matt. (2017). *Adlerian Psychotherapy: Theories of Psychotherapy Series,* Washington D. C. American Psychological Association

Cozolino, L. J. (2010). *The neuroscience of psychotherapy: Healing the social brain* (2nd ed.). New York, NY: W. W. Norton & Company.

Cozolino, L. J. (2015). *Why therapy works: Using our minds to change our brains.* New York, NY: W. W. Norton & Company.

Diamond, M. J. (2007). *My father before me: How fathers and sons influence each other throughout their lives.* New York, NY: W. W. Norton & Company.

Dilts, Robert. (1999) Sleight of Mouth: The Magic of Conversation Belief Change, California: Meta Publications

Dolan, M. Y. (1985). *A path with a heart: Ericksonian utilization with resistant and chronic clients.* New York, NY: Brunner/Mazel Publishers, Inc.

Erickson, B A., & Keeney, B. (Eds.). (2006). *Milton H. Erickson, M.D. an American healer.* Sedona, AZ. Chicago, IL: Ringing Rocks Press in association with Leete's Island Books Distributed by Independent Publishers Group.

Rosen, S. (Ed.). (1982). *My voice will go with you: The teaching tales of Milton H. Erickson, M.D.* New York, NY: W. W. Norton & Company.

Erickson, Betty Alice, Kenney, Bradford *Milton H. Erickson.M.D. An American Healer.* (2006) Scottsdale Arizona, Ringing Rocks Press

Erickson, M. H., & Rossi, E. L. (1981). *Experiencing hypnosis: Therapeutic approaches to altered states.* New York, NY: Irvington Publishers.

Erickson, M. H. (1980). *The collected papers of Milton H. Erickson on hypnosis* (Vols.1-4). Ernest L Rossi (Ed.). New York, NY: Irvington Publishers.

Erickson, M. H., & Rossi, E. L. (1979). *Hypnotherapy: An exploratory casebook.* New York, NY: Irvington Publishers, Distributed by Halsted Press.

Ewin, M. Dabne (2011). 101 things I wish I'd Known when I started Using hypnosis. Crown House

Fishbane, M. D. (2013). *Loving with the brain in mind: Neurobiology and couple therapy.* New York, NY: W. W. Norton & Company.

Fitzhugh, V. H. (2015, January 24) Naïve Prey Syndrome. (Web log poem). Retrieved from: https://cvillewinter.wordpress.com.

Flemons, D. G., & Gralnik, L. M. (2013). *Relational suicide assessment: Risks, resources, and possibilities for safety.* New York, NY: W. W. Norton & Company.

Gafner, G. (2010). *Techniques of hypnotic induction*. Bancyfelin, Carmarthen, Wales, UK: Crown House Publishing Limited.

Geary, B. B., & Zeig, J. K. (Eds.). (2001). *The handbook of Ericksonian psychotherapy*. Phoenix, AZ: Milton H. Erickson Foundation Press.

Gladwell, M. (2011). *Outliers: the story of success*. New York, NY: Back Bay Books.

Gottman, Julie Schwartz and Gottman, John. (2015) *10 Principles for Doing Effective Couples Therapy*, New York, NY: W.W. Norton and Company

Gottman, J. M. (2011). *The science of trust: Emotional attunement for couples*. New York, NY: W. W. Norton & Company.

Greenleaf, Eric. The Problem of Evil (2000) Phoenix, AZ. Zeig, Tucker and Theisen, Inc.

Hall, L. M., & Charvet, S. R. 2011). *Innovations in NLP for challenging times*. Bancyfelin, Carmarthen, Wales, UK: Crown House Publishing Limited.

Haley, J. (Ed.). (1985). *Conversations with Milton H. Erickson, M.D.* (Vols. 1-3). New York, NY: Triangle Press.

Hernandez, J. T. (2011). *Dialogues with pain: Internal body conversations that resolve suffering.* Bancyfelin, Carmarthen, Wales, UK: Crown House Publishing Limited.

Hernandez, J. L. (2013). *Family wellness skills: Quick assessment and practical interventions for the mental health professional.* New York, NY: W. W. Norton & Company.

Heschel, Abraham Joshua, (1995) *I Asked for Wonder.* Crossroad Publish Company New York.

Heschel, Abraham (2001) *The Prophets,* Harper Perennial

Hoorwitz, A. N. (1989). *Hypnotic Methods in Non-Hypnotic Therapies.* New York, NY: Irvington Publishers.

Hoyt, M. F. (2012). *Therapist stories of inspiration, passion, and renewal: What's love got to do with it.* New York, NY: Routledge.

Hoyt, M. F., & Talmon, M. (Eds.). (2014). *Capturing the moment: Single-session therapy and walk-in services.* Bancyfelin, Carmarthen, Wales, UK: Crown House Publishing Limited.

Kashdan, T., & Ciarrochi J. (2013). *Mindfulness, acceptance, and positive psychology: The seven foundations of well-being.* Oakland, CA: Context Press.

Kushner, Harold S. (2006) *Overcoming Life's Disappointments,* Alfred K Knopf, New York.

Lachkar, J. (2011). *How to talk to a borderline.* New York, NY: Routledge.

Lankton, S. (2004). *Assembling Ericksonian Therapy: The Collected Papers of Stephen Lankton.* Phoenix, AZ: Zeig, Tucker & Theisen.

Lankton, Stephen (1987) *Central Themes and Principles of Ericksonian Therapy,* New York, NY: Burner Mazel.

Lambrou, P. T., & Pratt, G. J. (2000). *Instant emotional healing: Acupressure for the emotions.* New York, NY: Broadway Books.

Lentz, J. D. (2014). *Double Binds: The DNA of emotional and mental problems and how to make use of their positive potential.* Jeffersonville, IN: Healing Words Press.

Lentz, J.D. (2012) *Compassionate Healing of Sex Addicts: And those who love them.* Jeffersonville, IN. Healing Words Press.

Lentz, J.D.(2002) How the Word Heals: Hypnosis in Scriptures, Writers Club Press. San Jose.

Lentz, J. D. (2016) *Tranceforming Bipolar: How to Help Folks Diagnosed with Bipolar Disorder Indirectly,* Jeffersonville, IN. Healing Words Press.

Lentz, J. D. (2011). *Trance altering: Epiphanies You can Create.* Jeffersonville, IN: Healing Words Press.

Lentz, J. D. (1986). *Effective handling of manipulative persons.* Springfield, IL: Charles C. Thomas Publisher.

Loriedo, C., Zeig, J. K., & Nardone, G. (2011). *Transforming Ericksonian Methods: 21st Century Visions.* Phoenix, AZ: Milton H. Erickson Foundation Press.

Lyons, Lynn (2015) *Using Hypnosis with Children: Creating and Delivering Effective Interventions,* New York, NY: W. W. Norton and Company

Madanes, Cloe', (1986) Behind The One-Way Mirror: Advances in the Practice of Strategic Therapy, San Francisco, Jossey-Bass Publisher

Meichenbaum, D. (2012). *Roadmap to resilience: A guide for military, trauma victims, and their families.* Clearwater, FL: Institute Press.

O'Hanlon, B. (2010). *Quick steps to resolving trauma.* New York, NY: W.W. Norton & Co.

Rosenfeld, S. M. (2008). *A critical history of hypnotism: The UNauthorized Story. United States of America:* Xlibris Corporation.

Rossi, Ernest L., Cheek, David, *Mind-Body Therapy Methods of Ideodynamic Healing in Hypnosis,* (1988) New York, NY: W.W. Norton and Company

Rossi. Ernest L. And Rossi, Kathryn. (2012) *Creating Consciousness: How Therapists Can Facilitate Wonder, Wisdom, Truth and Beauty.* Phoenix Arizona, Milton H. Erickson Foundation Press.

Schaler, Karen., *Travel Therapy: Where Do You Need to Go?* (2009) Berkley California, Seal Press.

Segur, Comtesse De, Sterrett Frances Virgina, *Old French Fairy Tales,* Philedephia, Penn Publishing Company.

Short, Dan. *Transformational Relationships,* (2010) Phoenix Arizona, Zeig, Tucker, Theisen

Short, Dan. Erickson Betty Alice, Klein, Roxanna Erickson, (2009) Hope and Resiliency:: *Understanding the Psychotherapeutic Strategies of Milton H. Erickson, MD.* Bethel, CT: Crown House

Siegel, D. J., & Solomon, M. F. (Eds.). (2013). *Healing moments in psychotherapy.* New York, NY: W. W. Norton & Company.

Siegel, Daniel J. (2016) *Mind: A Journey to the Heart of Being Human,* New York, W.W. Norton and Company

Simpkins, C. A., & Simpkins, A. M. (2010). *The dao of neuroscience: Combining Eastern and Western principles for optimal therapeutic change.* New York, NY: W. W. Norton & Company.

Simpkins, C. A., & Simpkins, A. M. (2012). *Zen meditation in psychotherapy techniques for clinical practice.* Hoboken, NJ: John Wiley & Sons.

Simpkins, C. A., & Simpkins, A. M. (2001). *Self-hypnosis plain and simple.* Boston, MA: Journey Editions.

Steere, D. A. (1982). *Bodily expression in psychotherapy.* New York, NY: Brunner/Mazel Publishers, Inc.

Steere, D A. (1989). *The supervision of pastoral care.* Louisville, KY: Westminster/John Knox Press.

Stoddart, K. P., Burke, L., & King R. (2012). *Asperger syndrome in adulthood: A comprehensive guide for clinicians.* New York, NY: W.W. Norton & Co.

Sugarman, L. I. (2014). *Therapeutic hypnosis with children and adolescents* (2nd ed.). Sugarman, L. I., & Wester, W. C. (Eds.) Bancyfelin, Carmarthen, Wales, UK: Crown House Publishing Limited.

Szasz, Thomas S. (1974) *The Myth of Mental Illness,* Harper and Row, New York.

Tarlow, T. (2012). *Clinical intuition in psychotherapy: The neurobiology of embodied response.* New York, NY: W. W. Norton & Company.

Tramontana, J. (2011). *Sports hypnosis in practice: Scripts, strategies and case examples.* Bethel, CT: Crown House Publishing Company LLC.

Walsh, B. (2008). *Utilization sobriety: A substance abuse solution.* United States of America: Peaceful Pilgrim Press.

Watzlawick, Paul, Bavelas, Janet Beavin, Jackson, Don. *Pragmatics of Human Communication; A Study of Interactional Patterns, Pathologies, and Paradoxes.* New York, NY: W.W. Norton and Company.

Wehrenberg, M. (2010). *The 10 best-ever depression management techniques: Understanding how your brain makes you depressed & what you can do to change it.* New York, NY: W. W. Norton & Company.

Westland Gill, (2015) *Verbal and Non-Verbal Communication in Psychotherapy,* New York, NY: W.W. Norton and Company

Wilkinson, Margaret. (2010). *Changing minds in therapy: Emotion, attachment, trauma, and neurobiology.* New York, NY: W. W. Norton & Company.

Yapko, Michael. *Mindfulness and Hypnosis: The Power of Suggestion to Transform Experience,* New York, NY: W. W. Norton and Company.

Zeig, Jeffrey K., *Ericksonian Methods: The Essence of the Story,* New York, NY: Bruner Mazel Company.

Zeig, Jeffrey K. (2014). *The induction of hypnosis: An Ericksonian elicitation approach.* Phoenix, Arizona: The Milton H. Erickson Foundation Press.

Zeig, Jeffery K. (1980). *A teaching seminar with Milton H Erickson.* New York, NY: Brunner/Mazel Publishers, Inc.

Zeig, Jeffery K. and Kulbatski, Tami. *Ten Commandments for Every Aspect of Your Relationship Journey,* (2012) Phoenix, AZ Zeig, Tucker, Theisen, Inc.

Zeig, Jeffery K. and Munion, Michael. *Milton H. Erickson,* (1999) London, Sage Publishing

Zeig, Jeffery K. (2015) *Psychoaerobics: An Experimental Method of Empower Therapist Excellence,* Arizona, Milton H. Erickson Foundation